DOT'S CORNER

"FROM MY HEART"

THE WRITINGS OF
Momma Doris
DORIS HOWARD SURLES

To order additional copies of this book, contact:
Xlibris Corporation
1-888-795-4274
www.Xlibris.com
Orders@Xlibris.com
49424

Contents

Family

Get Well

Inspiration

Journey Through Illness

Kids/Youth

Prayers

Stories

Cutie: A Mother's Day Gift for You

Thoughts of the Day

Words of Comfort

Thank You

Acknowledge and Dedication

To God be the glory—none of this would be possible without Him. To my mother, Mrs. Telsie B. Howard who kept me encouraged while she lived. For in God's vast universe one small corner is enough space for me to lift your heart and bring smiles to your faces.

To my Lord and Savior Jesus Christ, to the memory of my mother, the late great Mrs. Telsie B. Howard. Oh how I wish she could have seen this day. She would be so proud. To all of you for your inspiration, encouragement and dedication to me and this my lifelong project. I would like to dedicate this, my life's work, to all whom I hold so dear to my heart and that mean the world to me. So here it is—"Dot's Corner From My Heart." I pray that you will enjoy it, that it will bring you peace and that you will receive this book with the love and respect in which I wrote it. To my daughter, Gaynell Colburn, for her inspiration, for her encouragement, support and dedication to me and this my life's project. She has been with me throughout this project and without Gaynell I could not have gotten this done. Thank you for your designing eyes and bringing my book to life for me (smile my baby). I thank you for your contributions to this work and to me. Without you I could not have done this. I would also like to dedicate this to the Telsie B. Howard Foundation Inc., to my son Milton Hall, Jr. and his family, my Grandchildren, to Sisters Miss (Addie), Little Baby (Virginia), Little Sis (Mamie), to all my Brothers and Sisters that have gone before me, to my pastor Marshall Prentice and his lovely wife Elvira, to Colonel John Mann for believing in me and encouraging me to write this my first book as well as his lovely wife Jean, to my Storm, Stormetta Stateler, who has been with me from the beginning; working with me and Gaynell, using all her great gifts and skills as well as her fingers, eyes and that great mind (smile Storm). I thank you for your contributions to this work and to me. Without you I could not have done this. To my adopted family, to my dear Bishop Leroy Jackson Woolard. Thank God for you. To a very special niece and nephews, Charlie Ed and Verlean Howard, to Michael and to Larry I thank you for your contributions to this work and to me. Without you I could not have done this. To my Family especially my nephews and my very sweet nieces, to Staci, to my adopted family, to my sister friend Bea, Joyce, Terri, my Vitamins, and to my Church Family and to Stevie Wonder for his love of my daughter Gaynell and me his Momma Doris. There are so many others I have not room enough to mention all of the names. There are so many people who played such a major role in inspiring me to do this work I have not room enough to mention them all but to all of you as well I dedicate this book. May God bless you and keep you. I love you all. May you get this book, read it and enjoy it. Pass the word on so that others will also read it and be a part of "Dot's Corner".

I thank you from the very depths of my heart.

Hi, I'm Gaynell Colburn, the daughter of Doris Howard Surles. My mother's life's dream was to share this book with the world. Now the sad news I must share with you is that Mommy did not get to see this book come to fruition-to hold it. Although she had all the words written, it was not together for her to hold in her hands.

As she left me here alone, this has been the hardest thing I've ever had to do-to see that Mommy's life's work would still come to you.

I pray this Mommy's life's work, her writings, will be a great blessing to each and every one of you that read it. The Lord took my Mommy home, but her life, her words, her spirit, her love, and her dreams will still carry on. Through this book, share Momma Doris with everyone you know. This blessed work of God will be a blessing to them, too. It is with a heavy heart and through all my pain and total devastation; I smile when I see what my mother has accomplished. Please know that I need your prayers as I continue to bring her work to you.

There are more books to come. Be on the lookout for "What If" A test of Faith. One little quote from that book would be-What if this were you, would you stop praying or would you trust Him anyhow-how to get through terminal illness with total faith and trust in God. Mommy had unwavering faith.

This book was written in the hospital during her last days with her daughter, Gaynell Colburn.

MOMMY Mrs. Doris Howard Surles February 22, 1931-May 2, 2009

She went Home to be with The Lord after a long and devastating illness at 11:40 am from a terminal disease—Idiopathic Pulmonary Fibrosis. However, her faith never wavered. She leaned totally on The Lord. Mommy gave it all to God—she smiled Any How.

Mommy
It's me your baby girl
I love you more than anyone else in the whole world
You see you're my favorite girl
God gave you to me
He designed your heart you see just for me
To love me unconditionally
Mommy you are the best Mother in the world to me
I'm so blessed God saw fit to give you to me
The doctors say these are your last days but (God has the final say)
You have only a few months left to live
This breaks my heart and tears me apart
I know how much you love life and me
I know you want to live you have so much more to give
And how much more you want to do
When I think I will be without you
I don't know what to do or how I'll live
My whole life has been me and you
And everything I do is for you
Oh dear God what will I do without my greatest gift of all from you
You blessed me with this Mommy straight from Heaven Above
Filled with this special kind of love
You give from the heart
You love from the heart
Your food is cooked from the heart
Your heart is so big and so strong that everyone you know has a part
Your life has been filled with so many difficulties your life a struggle and
a fight you never let us know when you are low you are holding me up
But God brought you through "Any How" with a warm and loving smile
Mommy these are some of the things I would miss most of all
I would miss your smile
Your loving and healing touch
Your humor
Your resilience
Your hardy laughter
Our late night TV
We share everything just you and me
Our long rides together singing just you and me
We were always together and we always know where each other is

We always say I love you that is each and every day
A kiss good morning and a hug and kiss good night and a smile to get us
on our way
Mommy know I'm praying for you all night and all day
I wish everyone could have a Mommy like mine
You build me up and never ever put me down
Kept me humbled and rooted to the ground
You teach me to at all times have hope
To put the Lord first to pray and trust in Him only not in other folks
You feed me Jesus when I'm feeling spiritually, physically, mentally and
Financially low
You said trust in the Lord for everything and He will make it alright
Mommy you are my best and only true friend
Other than Jesus who's with me through thick and thin
I want to grow old with you Mommy like Granny and you
So I know what I have to do first of all know that God has got you
We know who has the answer we know who holds your hand
Mommy you've always been here for me
And Mommy our love has no end
So I'm asking the Lord for a miracle of healing just for you Mommy
Lord do this for me please I need my Mommy as she needs me she means
so much to me Lord my Mommy my friend. "Mommy" I love you
From your baby girl Gaynell
With all my love always "From the Heart"
Dedicated to my Mommy Mrs. Doris Howard Surles

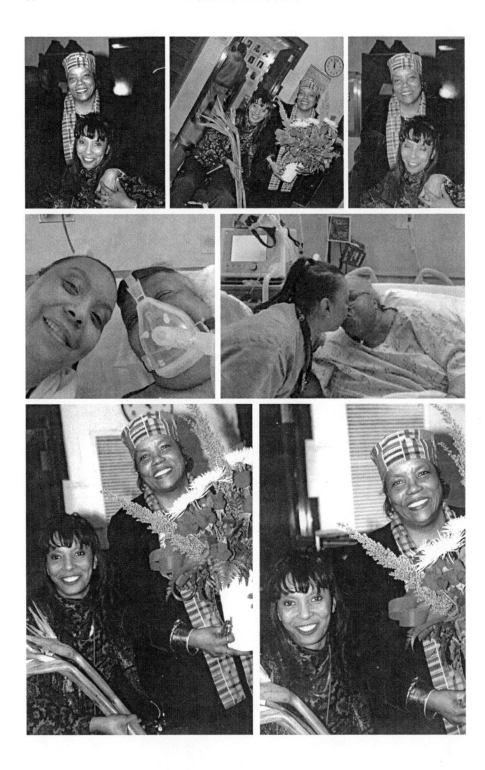

EXPRESSIONS, THOUGHTS AND FEELINGS

These are some of the feelings from my heart that I write as I ponder each day when I wake. I hope you enjoy reading them as much as I enjoyed writing them. I hope they help someone else through things they may be going through in their life.

A Letter to My Friend

My dear, sweet friend,
How can I express the joy and kindness
You have shown
During the good times and the bad
The ups and downs, the smiles and frowns
The happy times and the sad . . .
Today I received your beautiful letter
And your very timely card
That came, just when I felt the pain
Of loneliness and disregard.
My feelings were really on my sleeve
Though my faith had not been shaken
My body and mind had become weary
My intentions had been mistaken
I stopped everything and read the card
Then, I read your letter
But it's so good to have a Christian friend
To share what she has heard . . .
I guess you wonder why a poem
Well, my dear friend, it's because you're special
I could have written a long, long letter
Or called you on the phone
But, somehow I feel there's nothing quite like
A truly heartfelt poem
So before I end
May I say again
Your friendship means a lot to me . . .
Trust in the Lord with all your heart
Identify with Him each day
Never let Satan cloud or tarnish the gift God sent your way
Aggregate more of His faith and strength
Continue to share with others
Because you are truly blessed
To have the gift of caring for another
Every single word touched my heart
Right away, I felt much better . . .
My friend, I know God is in your life
I know, He sent you my way

It was as if you were standing
Right in front of me
Saying, look to Jesus today
My eyes filled with tears
My heart was touched
You could not have been sweeter
I opened my Bible and read the verses
You mentioned in your first letter
You said, you could not do much
To change my situation.
Oh, but you don't know
Just how much you eased my devastation
Every word you said is true.
I know the Lord
I know His word
And every day I thank Him
For a friend like you

A Love Note
To Someone Special
Instead of making phone calls
With lots of fancy words
Real feelings should be shown
As well as when in person
They are heard
Sweetie, or should I say my loved one
What do you suggest I do
Say lots of words
Read a bunch of lines
About what I'd like to say or do
Or do you suggest I show it
This is just how I feel about you

A Painful Decision

You never come in smiling
You say my home is a mess
I need to get rid of some this junk
When you come to see me you get depressed
How can you lift your eyes and pray
How can you make me feel this way
We do the best we can do
I could never say or do these things to you.
I've made up my mind
I'm not trying to be unkind
Tell you what I've decided to do
You call me from time to time and I'll call you.
If you can't help, don't make me feel bad
My life and home is not a loss
We'll get it together whatever the cost
If you come and feel in such an awful way
Then don't come I still love you and I'll be okay

A Yellow Rose
Why give my friend a yellow rose?
Could it be for a special reason well I suppose
Why present my friend with a yellow rose?
Could it be the fragrance, the beautiful color, or show one of God's mysteries unfold
There are many reasons I could proclaim
Let me just share a few that would mean the same
Admiration one reason I choose to give you the yellow rose
Love, loyalty, liberal, and many more traits I see in you
The yellow rose has many characteristics too
You take great pleasure in pleasing God, like the yellow rose in bloom
His world to you is like the aroma of precious perfume
You humbly hollow his Holy name
You are careful to give Him all praise
Like the thorns on the stem of the rose you don't hold back
No matter how hard
God's word like a banner you raise
You took an oath of obedience to the Lord, to observe and obey
Some obstacles will come your way
Just like the rose is protected by its thorns
So God's angels protect you night and day

An acceptable card

Cards are so beautiful, they often express how you feel and what you want to say

They have a way of brightening up your day

They remind you that someone is thinking of you.

Whatever the occasion may be

I receive many cards

But one exceeded them all

It was not fancy with legible writing with words of elegance

In fact it was wrapped with a rubber band.

You see this card was made for me, by a child that had no hands

It touched my heart so I cried there was nothing else I could do

This child held a pencil in its mouth and simply wrote

Hi I love you

So whenever I receive a card with words great or small I'm so grateful for every one

But this card exceeded them all

Don't Grandma Don't

Cry no more old Grandma
You're not one anyway
Just in name don't mean a thing
Why get blown away
Don't Grandma don't
You just can't get through your head
Maybe you'll be missed when you're dead
Put up your feeling
Dry up the tears you shed
Don't Old Grandma don't
I ain't no Grandma
Never was
Just used as one
Until something else occurred
I don't know why
I always worry
Don't Grandma don't
I wish I had a few tricks up my sleeve
As the old saying goes
Some magic way to get some caring
You know . . . just a little love
Don't do this Grandma don't

Enough is Enough
I think it's time for us to talk
I have waited much too long
I don't know why I hesitate
I need to know what's wrong.
I have known you all your life
I taught you how to walk
I was always there for you I even showed you how to talk.
I sang you songs, and you sang to me
I shared with you famous quotes
I introduced you to everyone I know
I even laughed at your not so funny jokes.
When you grew older I thought things would not change
I thought you would still be my little sugar cane
I somehow grew older too
I even admit I'm somewhat soft
I even allowed my sweetie to actually tell me off.
I don't mind you growing up
I don't mind if you must speak out
But I do mind being left out of your life
Without a shadow of a doubt
No matter what course in life you choose
My love will never change
No matter what you may be told to think
I'll love you all the same.
I think it is a terrible thing
To cut me out of your life
No hugs, no speaking, no conversations
It cuts my heart like a knife.
You are young now; you don't know how I feel
You won't even talk to me
You won't even answer my calls
This is not right
I cry day and night
You are not even keeping it real
How can you say I love you
You say I know the reason why
What are you waiting for tell me
Are you waiting for me to die

Don't let anyone fool you sweetheart
Time goes by so fast
You may not know or understand this now
But blood and love will last.
Why can't you let me in
We really have to fix this
God knows this is a serious issue
He knows this is a sin.
From my heart I will always love you even until the end

Fading Out
When darkness veils
And the storm prevails
Tears sometimes flow
My heart swells
My God . . . my God
What shall I do
Who on earth can I run to
I need a visible body to touch
I can't go it alone
It hurts too much
While I'm praying
What am I saying
I'm so troubled
I can't get through
My mind is racing
My thoughts are pacing
With so much pain . . . Lord
How can I talk to you
It's always a storm
In my life
I toss all during the night
People I love I cannot trust
We can't talk
We just invariably fight
I seemed to have lost . . . my faith and hope
I just exist from day to day
I need help now
I cannot go on
Help me find a way
I have tried
I have given
I have kept quiet
I even fuss
Nothing I do seems to be enough
Would it be better if I died
I don't know what else to do
Everybody seems so happy
When I start to talk

They refer me right to you
I don't say they are wrong
But right now I'm not strong
Relief is taking too long
Where and how do I find comfort
Show me where I went wrong
Every night I always say
Tomorrow will be a better day
This awful feeling that I'm carrying
Will surely go away
All I want is peace of mind
Just a little appreciation
Would be great
I work hard . . . I give and give
When do I get a chance to live
I cannot end this way Lord
It's just too hard with so many things gone bad
My days are dreary
My nights are tearful and sad
I'll just have to wait
To see what will happen now
One thing I do remember you said
You will make a way somehow
I am waiting . . . but I'm fading out

Feelings

Sometimes I'm so sleepy
I want to lie down too
I'd like to be with you alone
Like we used to do
But, can't you see what's happened
The way life takes a turn
I didn't expect this to happen
Believe me this is a burn
My heart is aching, my head is spinning
And I don't know what else to do
If you want to leave me
I certainly won't blame you
I promise I won't try to stop you
I won't lie, I'll be upset
But, I swear I won't be angry
I'll love you even yet

Feeling Blue

I'm lying round here with a cold watching some old movies
I wish I had myself a big bowl of sunshine
I was thinking as I take a sip of my herbal tea and honey
Where in the world can I get some money
But yet with all the things going wrong
Though I'm not in the pink
I still feel that a lot of things in life don't really stink
So I pick up myself from the couch
And thank God for a house, a family, and a dog

Footprints in the Sand
Isn't love wonderful
As my man said
My love and I can walk hand in hand
I love you so much
And I need you
These words I heard
From my man
Let me walk behind you
I can do this . . . I know I can
Put your footprints
In my pocket
Footprints you leave in the sand
Why pick up your footprints
Let them wash away with the tide
I must do this . . . not hide
With your footprints in my pocket
Keeps you always by my side
Oh how I love my man
Though he's no longer here with me
His physical body has gone
He left me alone
But there's a wealth of memories

Free

It has never happened
Someone or something is always attached
Keeps me bound hold me back
Loving others loving me I'll never forget
Being controlled never on my own
Chained, bound, yet secretly alone
Inward pain carrying shame
Afraid to express where to place blame
When will I be free

Happy Birthday
50 Years
If I had a card for you
I would have it say
I wish the very best for you
On this your 50th Birthday
I'd have it read all the things
We have shared throughout the years
As someone who knows and loves you
Talk about the joys, the laughter, and the tears
If I was there in person
This is what I would do
I'd sum it all up
By simply singing
The old favorite
Happy Birthday to you
So Happy Birthday, my dear heart,
And blessings from the Lord to you

Heart

If I had two hearts
I wouldn't mind if one was broken
If I had two hearts
I wouldn't mind if one was hurt by words that are spoken
If I had two hearts
One heart could bleed
While the other heart healed
If I had two hearts
One heart could take the pain
While the other heart be still
I could go on and on
For a long, long time
If I had two hearts
Yours and mine
But I only have one heart
God designed me this way
So I try to be very careful
Of the things I say and do
I have to think about
This heart of mine
And the heart that belongs to you
Since I have only one heart
A heart that's easily broken
I ask God to help make my heart strong
When evil words are spoken
When I see and hear evil things that are done
They tear and break my heart
You see . . . I have only one
Boy . . . am I a fool
Remember darling by this very same token
The one who breaks hearts
Will get their heart broken
Then you will say
In the very same way
I ain't nothing but a fool

How

How can I keep up?
Hold my head up
When you keep knocking me down
Treat me like I'm nothing
Even in a crowd
No recognition is ever found
When can I use the gift God gave me
If you keep holding me back
I'm not where I can push my way in
I've got to give respect

How Can This Be

How can you be so nasty
Hateful as you can be
Disrespect has become a way of life for you
Can you or someone explain this to me
How can you keep on prospering
While nice folk wish they could
The more you don't do
The more good things you get
You flaunt your bad behavior
And you have no regret
You look and act like
You don't care
You provoke anger anywhere
You bring out in others
Things they didn't know was there
How can this be
I can't compare
How can you explain
When you cause so much pain
Your insults fall like rain
Yet everyday good fortune
Comes your way
Is it goodness that just don't pay
People that carried you through the years
Are the very ones you bring to tears
You look at them and say oh well
In other words you can just go to hell
I got myself someone else
How on earth can this be
I figure the answer goes something like this
One day these people that care
You are going to really miss
Your good life is going to take a twist
Education and money won't mean a thing
Even your big car and your diamond ring
Yeah . . . you'll say Lord I'd give up everything
To do the right thing once again
How can this be

You might say
You think you know it all anyway
That's all I hear from you everyday
This is why I stay away
You may think that I'm a drag
You may think I just nag and nag
You may think I've turned into an old nagging hag
But you'll see
That's how its gonna be

I Ain't Nothing But a Fool

I thought I was hip
I thought I was cool
I thought I had you all figured out
Not one shadow of a doubt
But I found out I ain't nothing but a fool
I thought I really knew you
I thought no one knew you better
I thought I had you down to a "T"
Right down to the letter
Suddenly you have changed
All I seem to know now
Is your name
I can't tell you I'm lonely
Tired, crying, and sick
Just one phone call and you
Will leave me quick
I used to think that I came first
That love would come but not in a rush
I thought no matter who you met
You wouldn't leave me alone
At least not yet
A new life you discovered
But I thought you would
Give me a chance to recover
Not throw me away and go have your fun
Not once in awhile
But every day
I hope when from this cloud
You come down
The one you hurt will still be around
To catch you before you hit the ground
I hope the pain won't hit
You square in the face
When someone comes along
And takes your place

I Am Gone

I am alone . . . gone
On a mental flight
Into the night
Yet darkness is not around
In fact it's morning
There's not a cloud in sight
What is taking me into this dark hole
Oh God . . . I'm burning up
Yet I'm so cold
I'm dizzy from spinning
But I'm sitting still
I cannot explain how I feel
This may be insane
But I have sense enough
To identify my pain
I want to go back into my dark place
It's scary but I feel secure and safe
It's quiet yet I can't shut out the sounds
I'm surrounded by voices
But then there's no one around
I am here and there
I'm sick and well
I know there is Heaven and I'm aware of Hell
I am able to read that I can't even spell
I am who I am . . . I am what I am
I am where I am
Confused? Misused? Abused?
I am . . . I am . . . I am

I Am Me and You

I see me I dream you
I know who I am
And I want to be you
I am young and old
I am shy and bold
I am hot and cold
I am me and you . . .
Which one are you
Are you able to say
Do you dream like me every day
Are you me at night
When no one sees
Are you, you, or are you me
I am happy and sad
I am a little good
A whole lot bad
I long for me
Yet it's you I wish I had . . .
I am woman and girl
Shivering with thoughts
That makes my head whirl . . .
I want your youth
Your body
Your mind
I want me to know
Each and every time
You make my sunshine
Yes I am you and me . . .

I Can't Get God's Forgiveness Until I Have Forgiven You
Child do you remember one Sunday
It was about a year ago, maybe two
How she sat there and rolled her eyes at me
I still think about it don't you
I just can't stand that woman
No matter what she do
And I ain't gonna never forgive her for that
Well sister . . . God won't forgive you
I was sitting right here in church one night
I think you and me had just met
You saw her deliberately bump right into me
I tell you I ain't forgot that yet
Now I know right well she saw me
Because she stepped all on my shoes
I was just about mad enough to hit her
But I remember the golden rules
I never forgave her for that hateful act
It was a nasty thing to do
Well . . . sister you had better start
Asking right now
Because God will not forgive you
Oh . . . what about the time I paid my dues
Just about every cent I had
She pretended she forgot to read my name
It was written right on her pad
I tell you she's got it in for me
I'll just feed her with a long handle spoon
She had better not talk about forgiving her
Well sister in the sight of God
You are doomed
Wait . . . I just want to tell you this
And then I'll let you go
This sister I'm talking about
Is right in church
If I call her name you would know
She even mistreats my children
She is jealous of what I wear
She talks about everything I do

I tell you it ain't no love there
Anytime she sits and whispers about me
Trying to get others on her side
I ain't got nothing else to say to her
If I live to be a hundred and five
Now don't get me wrong . . . I ain't mad at her
'Cause I am holy deep down inside
I'm gonna just keep away from her
If she comes to my house I'll hide
If we are on the same side of the street
I just cross to the other side
Honey, I'm gonna just sit back and watch her
While she wallows in her selfish and foolish pride
Now sisters, you stop fooling yourselves
Let Jesus come into your hearts
Go to each other . . . get your things right
Then ask forgiveness from God
There is not one way to get around it
It is written in his Holy Word
Until you have forgiven
Your sisters and brothers
Your prayers will not be heard
Now when we ask the Lord to forgive us
Remember dear sisters and brothers
We cannot get through to God in prayer
Until we have forgiven each other

I Miss Mother

I

If I could hear my Mother pray again
And tell me the story of how Jesus saved her from sin
She told me of God's love and His saving grace
In my mind I can still see her smiling face

Chorus
I miss my Mother . . . oh yes I do
I miss her sweet smile
I can still hear her saying
I miss you my child, but I'm not worried . . . one day I will see her
(Yes I'll see her again)
On those streets of gold
We'll walk together with Jesus
Forever . . . forevermore

II

Mother that still hears
Though sometimes maybe hard . . . but I know we can make it (yes we can)
If we just trust in God
We've got to keep on believing
In Jesus be strong
He will keep us together
Safe in His arms

III

If you still have your mother
You ought to love her everyday
Because you never, never, never know
When death will snatch her away
Oh when her body, when her body lay in a cold, cold grave . . . there's nothing
you can do for her
Nothing can be said

Special Chorus
Tell her everyday
I love you Mother in a special way
Give her flowers . . . honor her . . . pray for her

And with a great, great smile
Say Mother I thank God for you and I am so glad so glad so glad to be your child
Oh I still miss my Mother
I miss her smile
In my mind I can still hear her saying I love you my child
But one day I'll see her
On those streets of gold
We'll be happy together forever more

IV
To the Mothers that are still here
Though some times are hard
I know we can make it
If we just trust in God
Keep on believing
In Jesus be strong
We can make it together
We are safe . . . oh He'll keep us safe in His arms

I Remember
Tell a Child
I remember you my child
You were so much fun
How you loved to jump and bounce
You were loved by everyone
I remember the coos and giggles
The things that gave you joy
Counting fingers and toes
How you wiggled your nose and reaching for a toy
You never cried very much
Except when you were wet
You always waited for that tender touch and big hug around the neck
I remember from the time you were born
Until this very day
I knew you were a blessing from God
In a very special way
You were such a joy

I See You
You think I only find
Fault in you
Well you are wrong
I see good things you do
You think I forgot
How you were here for me
Telling me you're going to be fine
Just wait and see
I thought I put it all
In your great big card
You think I forgot
That would be very hard
You are sweet (sometimes)
Cute as can be
You're my Bubbling Brown Sugar
Are you smart? Definitely
You will always be
Not one but three
Brown Sugar, Puddin' Pie, and even
Sugar to me
I'm happy because
No one can take
You away from me
Yes, I am to you
What they can never be
I see you
I remember your tears
When I did something nice
When I calmed your fears
When I gave you a hug
And say you did good
I miss all that
I wish I still could
You can make me laugh
At least you used to
You tickled me with the silly things
You used to do
We would go for a ride

Or just stay inside
You and I had fun
And we were alive
We made stupid sounds
We fooled around
We ate and looked at tapes
We played games
Mentally our ages were the same
So don't think I don't see the niceness in you
What makes you think
I don't see
Why do you think I act so crazy
I don't want to let you go
I miss you and the times we had
I see my dear sweet playmate
And all the good
I'm just so sad
You make my heart hurt

Keep on Singing . . . Stop Complaining

Sing over me when I'm gone
But while I'm living help me be strong
Sing me a song about ones there
But show me love while I'm here
Sing a song about how Jesus cares
But stop fussing and fighting
While I'm here
You get angry with me
You disagree with me
Not knowing when I might die
When you get the news will you refuse
To sing "Savior, Don't Pass Me By"
Will you miss me or say . . . she's finally gone
Will you cry or will you sing "Oh Happy Days"
Or "In the Sweet Bye and Bye?"
Will you sing "Never Alone"
To family and friends
When you have not been kind
Will you sing "The Joy of The Lord Is My Strength"
Or my favorite song "Yes, Jesus Is Mine"
"Friendship with Jesus" is what we sing
"Fellowship Divine" that may be what we croon
We know that hatred is cruel as the grave
We fuss . . . we scream
We even swear about almost anything
Then we put on our robes with no regrets
Singing "Glory To His Name"
You look down on me
You cry again and again
But when I was living
It was grief and pain
Listen to yourself saying all those beautiful things
Things I would love to hear
When I was living you did not bother
Nor did you seem to care
Come on . . . let's stop the foolishness
Right now, come as one and agree
No one can stop love but you and me

Whatever is lost or bound on earth
The same will be in Heaven
I love you all right here right and now
For all my wrongs I've been forgiven
Now we all can sing God's Heavenly songs
We'll meet and greet in Heaven

Life

When I think of my life and how I feel
It's sometimes hard to explain
There are times when words cannot express it
There are times when I care not to confess it
It's so intimate, so intolerable, so restrained
My life is a mixture of emotions
Emphasized by pitfalls and pains
Spiritless and stripped by suspicions
Susceptible to the tempest it brings
Melancholy, more than I'll ever admit
Fantasies I wish were real
Bashful yet appearing at ease
Hidden and suppressed anger is what I feel
Lord, what is over forty
I am not old, I haven't grown cold
What can it be, will I ever be free
Am I too old for hot pants
Too young for old slacks
Too old to go forward
Too young to stay back
Can't wear size eight to ten
Can't squeeze in nine to twelve
A little comfortable in size eighteen
Most times feel like hell
Sometimes happy, more times sad
Try to say something good
It just turns out bad
Walk a block out of breath
Can't seem to stop eating
Sometimes I can't stand myself
I have skills, knowledge from the past
Yet doing nothing positive that will last
I have good sense I don't always use
Even my talents I sometimes abuse
Sometimes I wonder, what's the use
If this was your life
What would you do

Listen to the Voice
When skies are blue
I didn't need you
Everything was going my way
I could visit the fields
And smell the flowers
I had no bills to pay
A quiet voice whispered
Don't forget about me
I'm the one who made the sun
It is I who keep the skies blue
I give the strength to walk the fields
I would never forget you
The sound of fun and laughter
Was all I listened to then
I chose to have fame and fortune
The crowd I sought to win
That quiet voice kept after me
No matter where I would go
On every street, in every room
It just would not go away
Come to me, I want you
The voice said . . . I am the door
I continued on for years and years
Refusing to obey the call
The more I tried to pretend
Whether in a crowd or all alone
The voice came again and again
Then one day, the blue skies turned gray
Nothing was going my way
There were no more fields and flowers
I had a debt to pay
My bills were past due
My friends were less than few
No more joy and laughter I found
That is when I started crying
I felt like dying, every smile became a frown
Then, I heard that quiet voice again

This time, I listened . . . I had no choice
It spoke as soft as a soothing wind
The voice said . . . I brought you here to make you aware
When all else fails, I am still your friend

Me Being Honest and Real

Oh I sure would love to be well known famous; recognized by important people. When I pick up a book and see pictures or a list of names, writings or quotes, I certainly would like to be listed there when the pastor gets up to speak or preach and he looks my way, calls my name or mentions my name or a song I might have sang. Oh, that feels good.

I am so grateful when it comes to being loved accepted or noticed by others, whether it's family or not—no matter the race or sex or age. I'm not content just being me. It seems I am just blessed when I can be called mama, mommy, auntie, sister, or some nickname that makes me more than just my birth name. You would be amazed how often I have cried. I mean broken hearted when I am or feel that I'm excluded or not included as a part of a family especially when I have been told I am family. When there is an event like a family reunion, a special trip, a home going, a wedding, a christening, or a family discussion. I have a real problem with these things.

My Secret Sin
I have a secret sin I can tell no one
Keeping it is very hard
I'm ashamed and afraid
It follows me everywhere
It always surfaces I believe on purpose
Every time I go in prayer
I told God about my sin
Of course He already knew
I asked Him please forgive me
Yet it haunts me more than ever before
This is not my secret sin
That is so hard to share
It's about how I feel
This sin could kill someone I hold so dear
Should I continue in this sin
The Bible says God forbid
Then what can I hope to accomplish
If my secret sin remains hidden
Oh, how terrible it would be
When I am heaven bound
If my secret sin is kept
And I lose my heavenly crown
Is it really in the sea of forgetfulness and remembered no more
If this is true, why then do I feel trapped
I'm tossing to and fro
Is it worth the risk
Or the joy I miss
Keeping my secret sin
Please tell me Lord, this is so hard
Each day holding it within
Then the Lord spoke very clear
Your secret sin you told to me
It is not yours anymore
When you asked me to forgive you, immediately I remembered it no more
My child you can't forgive your sin
I am the only one
When I cried, when I died
The work's already done

So open your heart
See, the sin is gone
Go on and pray
You told me your wrong
No one else need ever know
I am the door worry no more
I will keep you safe and strong

My Needs
I need someone to hear me
I need someone to touch
I need someone to count on
Oh, I need so much.
I need someone to be a mother
I need a father, too
I need a friend to be there for me
Could that someone be you
I need someone to love me
Not just physically
I need someone to understand
Even when I'm just silly
I need someone to depend on
And when I need it to defend
I need someone regular
Not just now and then
I need someone to stand by me
Even when I'm wrong
I need someone that knows my weaknesses
And help me to be strong.
I need someone to comfort me
Let me share my ups and downs
I need someone to make me laugh
Even when I frown
Wow, I have so many needs
I wonder what I can do
I guess I'll just keep going around
Until I've found that someone like you.

My Walk Through the Valley
As I walk
Through the valley of sickness
The valley of pain
The valley of poverty
No earthly gain
The valley of unacceptance
The valley of harm
The valley of crime
No rights only wrongs
The valley of rejections
The valley of despair
The valley of loneliness
Is there anyone who cares
When I walk through the valley
Will you go with me there
Walk with me if you dare

My Gift

I was very sad today
Because I had no gift to give
I never thought to thank the Lord
Just for letting me live
I was really broken up
About the things I could not buy
I didn't stop to think about Jesus
And that it was for me He came to die
I was ashamed and embarrassed
When I didn't have all the beautiful things
Clothes, toys, cars, even houses
And diamond rings
What can I give for Christmas
At least one gift from me
I don't have anything to put under the Christmas tree
Not only that, but I wouldn't like to have not one, not two, or three
What can I do this Christmas
I don't want others to think I'm cheap
After all I had one whole year
To give family and friends a treat
I looked and searched and thought
Then I began to cry
How could I be so forgetful
About that bright star in the sky
How could I forget the Wise Men
The manger and the hay
How could I forget that Christmas
Is His birthday
How could I forget that Jesus
Is the greatest gift of all
He gave Himself to all the world
From the moment He was born
I thank Him for what He gave me
My heart, my soul, my mind

Note of Cheer
Happy Birthday
Full of fun and laughter
Is what I want for you
Reaching for the stars
In whatever you do
Enduring with patience all
The ups and downs
Doing the right thing
Don't let anything turn you around
Always remember, wherever you may be
Always remember whatever comes your way
I'm with you and I love you
Today and everyday
This is your special day

Pity

Oh poor, poor, poor
Little pitiful me
No one else is suffering
Like me you see
I have no time to give good news
I am far too busy crying the blues
I got swollen feet, lips and face
I rate myself a total disgrace
Needles and pills, sweats and chills
Aches and pains, no more thrills
Then along came one of my friends
That I had not seen for awhile
Remember me my friend said
Oh it hasn't been that long
You forgot my name is smile
I brought you something
Very special this time
It's only one of a kind
I opened it and said
What is this
Oh look, it's a beautiful
Bottle of sunshine
Well, said smile and sunshine
We travel from city to city
And as soon as we got your name
We came to help you knock out pity
So I got a pen and began to
Write and read
I even held back a scratch and a sneeze
As I kept on reading and began to write
I know I would have no trouble
With old pity tonight
Now if by chance
You are feeling low
Just stop for a minute
Take it slow
Stop by and see me
Before you go

I'll make sure
You won't have pity no more
Tucked away inside my heart
I have lots of sunshine
Take some, don't worry
I have plenty
Go ahead take all you want
Pass them around to everyone
And they don't cost you a penny
This I wrote while in Good Samaritan Hospital Intensive Care. I was feeling low.

So In Love
So in love, this cannot be
Must be somebody else
Certainly it's not me
Well, I should have known
After all I'm grown
It hurts so bad when you get stung
Especially when it's by someone so young
Some may say you know better
You got just what you deserve
You're always falling for the wrong one
Then you got kicked to the curb
Everyone expects me
To be so brave and strong
Why can't I be weak sometimes
Why shouldn't I be hurt when I'm treated wrong
You step on me, you call me names
Then you leave me all alone
But one day you'll be sorry
When you return and no one is home
Then you will cry to the Lord above
Please send me someone
For I'm so in love
I meant someone special, Lord
Someone sent from above

To a Friend

Promises you believe are made to be kept
Associates are many yet few
Yielding sometimes not often
Never regretting doing whatever you must do
You are equal to any, second to none
A friend whenever you can be
This my idea of a true friend and a star
This is to you my friend from me
The many things you do for others
Truly makes you a star
Doing whatever little or much
And this is very rare by far
Envious you never seem to be
Rich with charm and personality
Liberal lively an unchangeable love
What a gift from God above
Each day you encourage someone
You know I really believe
A friend like you feels real good
When your day is done

What About Me

Why do you make me feel so bad
About things I cannot change
Why do you break my heart
About things I cannot explain
Give me a reason or show me a way
I can help you to be kind
Don't just see the things you want
Help others some happiness to find
Why must I always ache
Because you feel so bad
Why can't you see and understand
Without always getting mad
Sometimes you make me feel stupid
Because I want to help
Sometimes things are forced on me
Things I don't create myself
If I could only get you to see
That things don't go my way
I don't know why I'm always chosen
To make someone have a better day
I love you more than anyone
Even more than I love myself
Seeing you unhappy
Is almost as bad as death
I hope someday, somehow, someway
You will try to accept me and my ways that seem so strange
And pray that if it's God's will
He will help me change my ways

What About Me

How come I'm not heard?
How come I can't speak?
Why can't I be forgiven?
Why am I so weak?
Why do I keep doing wrong?
What happened to my power?
Something keeps telling me to do it
Every day and every hour
Every time I say I'm right
There is no harm in this
Then before I know it
I've gone and done it again
I took the wrong risk
What about me
This is some of the things I see
I can do better
When I take a good look at me

What Do You Say Love Is
What is love
The Bible tells you and Webster has its meaning
So what do you say love is
When you think of me as a jewel
When you forgive me
When you see me beautiful inside and out
When you can cry with me
When you can lift me when I fall
When you love me so much you can look
Into my eyes and see my love
With a great sense of pride
Some may say that's not true
But when you love someone the way I do
You can look into their eyes
The windows of their soul
And know what love is

What If

*What if I had someone to encourage me when I was growing up.
Someone to tell me you are going to be alright when the going was
rough . . . When I went to school and couldn't do my work. What if
someone would reach out and help me. So I wouldn't feel like a stupid
jerk. When I felt alone Mama wasn't home what if a little love and
attention were shown. Instead of being called out of my name feeling
ashamed and for so many things I would get the blame.*

*What if when I went to church to hear Jesus joy bells ring. Why couldn't I
even get a compliment when I stood to sing . . . . I wanted love. I wanted
help. I wanted to feel good about myself. I wanted to stand tall and special
at school, church, and home. Sometimes I would ask myself, why was
I born. Now that I'm grown I still feel alone. I wonder if others can tell. I
guess not because I hide it so well. If people around could see inside they'd
see what I always hide, my smiles are frowns and my true feelings are all
dressed in pride. What if I put pen to paper. I feel deprived. Writing seems
to bring out what I really feel. It's amazing to me to know how much these
things are so very real. What if my relationships had been good. Are my
friendships genuine and true. What if I find I've been deceived not once
but many, many times . . . . Life goes on so people say and life doesn't go
my way. So through God I'm saved today so I thank him, what if, what if.
Someday, all my questions will be answered.*

What If

What if I wake up and find that what I thought is life is all a dream, no human existence, no name, children, pain, sound all a dream no reality at all. Suppose I am an imagination, every move a make believe. Friends and love ones all made up in a make believe mind, a fading thought. What if I could change the pattern to suit me.

What is My Purpose
What is my purpose in life
I seem to be useless
It seems as if life is just
Passing me by
It seems to me everyone I talk to or see
Whether in person, in passing or on TV
Is so busy so happy, so content and they have
So many meaningful things to do
I want to be useful, special and needed
What am I to do beside cook and clean
Lord, what am I supposed to do?
Who am I?
Where do I go to be gainfully employed
I see people in church, happy, busy
And useful in various ministries
I say to myself, I can do that
I see people on TV singing, writing
Speaking and telling stories
Again I say to myself, I can do that.
So why am I not doing these things
Why don't I seem to fit in
How do I get started
Who do I turn to for answers
I wrestle with this
I have skills
Everyone seems to be too busy to take time
Everyone seems too occupied with their busy schedule to take notice of how
I'm hurting
Who can help me
Then I realized the answer is right here, right in my hands
As the saying goes, right under my nose
When I ask these questions and I expressed my concerns, I was alone
Or so I thought
Jesus said, "The Holy Spirit spoke, you serve me"
Oh, but I do Lord. I serve you everyday
Again He spoke "Serve me."
You worship me, but I want you to serve me
How, Lord? I answered, How?

He said, To serve me is to trust me
To trust me is to take me totally in your confidence
No doubt as to who you are
You are my child. Haven't I cared for you?
Even before you knew me, I knew and know you
Just serve me, trust me, learn of me, rely on me, lean on me
Ask me and I will show you where you belong
Take your eyes off who's who and look at me
See me in you. See me in my word. Hear me when I speak
Hear what my Spirit says. Hear me. Stay in my word. I will show you
where you belong, what your calling is, how to use the gifts and talents I have
given you and when to use them
Thank you, Lord for opening my eyes and understanding.
What greater gift, what greater joy, what greater duty than to be a servant
of the Lord

When I Sing

I have the love of Jesus in my soul
When I sing
It seems the billows cease to roll
When I sing
A little wheel just starts a burning
When I sing
The spiritual fire just starts a burning
When I sing
More and more my heart is yearning
When I sing
All praise and glory to God our king
I can hear the joy bells ring
I want the world to know He is my everything
When I sing
The love of God is so real
When I sing
I can communicate with my Lord
When I sing
Trials can be high as mountains
Troubles like a raging sea
They just disappear nothing bothers me
When I sing
No wonder the birds sing so early in the morning
And fly so high and free
Like the birds I feel happy and free
Rich as a king
When I sing
Oh what peace and joy I find
When I sing
Nothing troubles my mind
When I sing
God is my voice
Jesus is my melody
The Holy Spirit is the breath I breathe
No credit belongs to me
When I sing
Let me ever lift my voice

Let this always be my choice
That every race, sex, color and creed
Be one united like a loving ring
When I sing

Why

Why can't I get thru my head
Why in God's name up above
Why do I keep on trying
To understand real friendship and real love
Why is blame always placed on me
No matter what I say
Why am I so misunderstood
Why do people come along and take a loved one away
Why do I think you ever loved me
Or could ever be my friend
All I ever wanted in life
Is to be loved through thick and thin
Age never mattered much to me
Whether it is woman or man
Why do I reach out with all my heart
To be hurt again and again
Where did I go wrong
I never forced myself on anyone
All I did was opened my arms
I know it has not been that long
How can you lose someone so fast
Why can't I see and not hide the truth
If it is real, then it will last.
Why do I feel I've been cheated
Just when I think all is well
Why do I feel mistreated
I'm hurting and there is no one I can tell
When I mixed my blood with your blood
I didn't do it as some little child
I took it very sincerely
I sealed it with a hug and a smile
Why do you enjoy hurting me with insults and sneers
You even call me names
In just a few months
You've thrown everything away
You make me feel dirty and ashamed
There's no one on earth I love more
That's why I sometimes say bad things too

I know I should have had more control
But it's because I still love you
You think I talk and say bad things about you
You think I've gone in with some others
You think I don't want you to have friends or fun
Or I try to be another
I don't think you really know what damage you have done
You say I think I know everything
You say I think I'm always right
You say I won't let things go
Why don't you think love is worth the fight
Please don't think this is about physical love
That's my least concern
I'm asking what about heartfelt love
A lesson we all can learn
It's hard for you to see it now
Let me tell you some reasons why
You're young and you think you'll never die
You got a place to go and stay all day
Even half the night
Free food and free hair dos
So you feel you're doing all right
You don't need my little affection
You got a man to comfort you
One you can wrap around your little finger
And do what you want him to do
You got yourself thinking
As you said I'm old
I'll only slow you down
You are very happy and content
Not having me around
I talked to you and cried to you
And shared all my woes
It's something I had to do
I had to share with others my pain
It wasn't to pull them away from you
I know they don't care how I feel
You show them kindness that you don't show me
The things you do when they are not around

Are the things you don't let them see
Why do you see me so different now
Why you make me feel like dirt
Think about all the times we spent
Helping you get rid of your hurt
The worst thing I could or would ever do
Is change on you this way
Why do you seem so happy
Don't you know this will haunt you someday
Why can't you see how dangerous this is
Not to answer to anyone
You leave and no one sees or hears from you
Until the day is done
Why can't I ask you anything
Without you getting so up tight
Is it sex, kisses or more this sudden twist
It just doesn't seem right
No matter how much they give you
It's just not worth the risk
To give up everyone who loves you, Just for thrills and your stubbornness

Yellow Roses
Why give my friend a yellow rose
Could it be for special reasons
Well I suppose
Why present my friend with a yellow rose
Could it be the fragrance
The beautiful color
Or to show one of God's mysteries unfold
There are many reasons
I could proclaim
Let me just share a few
That would mean the same
Admiration is one reason I chose
To give you the yellow rose
Love, loyalty, and liberal and many more traits I see in you
The yellow rose has many characteristics, too
You take great pleasure in pleasing God
Like the yellow rose in bloom
His word to you is like the aroma of precious perfume
You humbly hollows His holy name
You are careful to give Him all praise
Like the thorns on the stem of the rose
You don't hold back no matter how hard
God's word like a banner you raise
You took an oath of obedience to the Lord
To observe and obey
Obstacles will come
The rose is protected by its thorns
So God's angels protect you night and day

FAMILY

My Family means so much to me, they are loved so much. There are not words enough to express all the love I have from my heart, oh how I love them with all my heart.

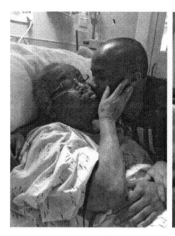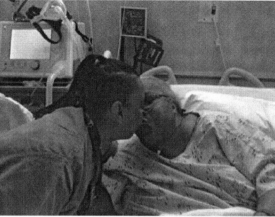

You see "Mommy" Ma, Grandma, Mimi, Momma Doris and Auntie is Loved so very much by so very many we love you. You are the heart beat of the family.

A Family Reunion
To The Entire Family
When we first heard about this family reunion
We were as happy as could be.
But we are more excited
Than you could ever know
For making us a part of this blessed event
Is well worth waiting for,
We pray that God will bless
Each and every part
Keep safe the family and the friends
With love and oneness of heart,
We are here to help in anyway
Enjoy this celebration
To offer our sincere support
Without the slightest hesitation,
God Bless

A KISS FROM MOMMY

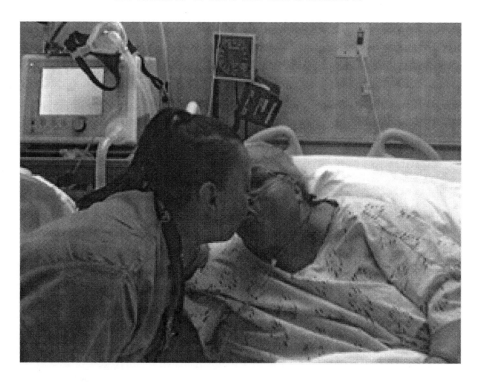

A kiss from Mommy—you'll never know how much this means to me. It wasn't just the kiss, it was her show of love to me. Mommy, I would give anything in the world for just one more kiss from you. My life and my heart are so empty now that you are gone. If I could just have one more day to show you just how special you are to me. I never took your love for granted. Every day we spent together was a special day. So many nights I held you in my arms. We cried together, we prayed together, we laughed together and we stayed together. Somehow even that doesn't seem to be enough for me. I pray that what I gave from my heart to you was good enough. I wanted to be the best daughter in the world for you because you were the best Mommy in the world to me. So when I went through my worst times, a kiss from you would always make my day because it came with so much love and compassion. There are no words that can explain. You would look me in my eyes and tell me that everything is going to be just fine. It's going to be alright you said and as long as you were with me it was. Without you Mommy my world has been turned upside down. I can't seem to get myself together, Mommy, but if I could have a kiss from you I know I would be okay. The nights are long and lonely. Without a kiss from Mommy I am slowly dying. I can't stop crying. My heart hurts, my mind is messed up, my life will never be the same. I struggle every day to try to go on without my Mommy. I need to hear the sound of her voice, see her smile, feel the love and the sweet loving kindness Mommy gave to me and all those she loved. It wasn't just a kiss from Mommy. It was the love she poured into me each and every day of my life. I don't know how I'll go on. Nothing is right. Everything is going wrong. I find it hard to go on. I know I sound like I have no faith, but when a Mommy like mine, who was my best and closest friend is gone, your heart, your world, your life and everything as you knew it is no longer the same and you are facing total devastation. People need to give me the love, support and time to learn how to go on without the loving kindness and support that she gave me every day and all the time. Mommy and I were never apart. We are a part of each others' heart. We did everything together. I look for her. I reach for Mommy in the night. I always took care of her. I never left her side. I miss sitting at Mommy's hospital bedside laughing, talking and looking at TV all night. We also cried. We prayed for mercy. We read the Bible every night. I'm hurt and in so much pain. I miss you Mommy. I can't eat, can't sleep and I lost my smile-the smile only you could bring out of me and was just for you.

Mommy, this kiss means so much to me-more than anyone could know. We never got too busy to show each other how much we loved one another every day. There is always a kiss good night and a kiss good morning and lots and lots more kisses throughout the day. Because you are such a loving and kind Mommy, these words are effortless to say because Mommy you are love and you show it day by day. Oh, by the way Mommy your kiss would last me all day.

Mommy you poured so much in to me with your kiss, your smile, your loving kindness, and your faith that never wavered. You fed me Jesus and taught me how to be an anyhow person, and even though I'm facing total devastation I know that all the work you did on me all my life will not be in vain. I know in my heart that if I keep looking, praying, listening, and keeping the faith as I walk through these dreary days, the Lord will grant me that one more kiss that I've been longing for from Mommy.

From your baby girl Gaynell
With love always "From my Heart"
Dedicated to my Mommy Mrs. Doris Howard Surles

A Sister

Hi my sister
I thought about getting a card
With a lot of fancy words
Written by someone else
With expressions I didn't prefer
You my sister, is what I always knew
Since I was a little girl
I always admired you
Mama did a good thing
When she brought you into the world
Now that we are grown ups
It's as plain as can be
You know how special you are
Because you never forget about me
You send me beautiful cards
That always gives me a lift
And inside every single card there is always a special gift-
I just thought I would let you know
How much you mean to me
I am so proud that you are my sister
And this is for you
Sincerely with love
Your sister Doris

A Tribute to My Sister Miss

Addie

A - Admirable, Admired and Appreciated by me, your baby sister, Doris
D - Delightful, Decisive, Dedicated to the Lord and her family
D - Determined, Deeply loved by all, especially me and her family
I - Inspirational, Incredible,
E - Enduring, Earnest, willing worker for the Lord

I couldn't ask for a finer sister though all of my sisters are fine. But in my heart and in my mind I know that this sister of mine, Addie Roles, is a woman of God that put Him above all else.
When I think of Miss, I think of smile you kept me laughing we had the greatest times. When I think of you I think
"Miss"
Mission minded, meticulous,
Interesting, a unique and
Sweetly saved sister
Sensational
Mirror, mirror on the wall who's the fairest and finest of them all?
Addie Roles, Addie Roles
I love you and have a blessed birthday.
May the Lord bless and keep you forever in His care.

With love
Your baby sister,
Doris

A Son

See the bears on your card my son
I chose them for a reason
Bears are tough, intelligent, and very strong
Bears have their problems
But they get along
They have their times, when they
Growl and fight, but they forgive
And make up before the night
Sometimes Papa Bears do a lot of hugging
Even stray but he comes right back to Mama Bear
He don't stay away
They are always there for their cubs
When Papa Bears teach them how to behave
They are patient and gentle as doves
Son if Papa Bear, Mama Bear and Baby Bears
Who are animals get along
Don't you know God will take
You as His children In His loving arms
Don't you know He will teach you
No matter how young or old
He wants you to be happy and
Protect from the cold
He made you son, so special
Created you, with His own hands
Gave you knowledge and wisdom
He calls this the master plan
Love your family
I believe you do
So ask the Lord to reprogram you
And show you how to be
Big and strong as the bear
Wise as the bumble bee Gentle and strong as the bear
Take charge of His plan, you are the man
Take control, but do it with God's love
Every day give gentle bear hug
Mommy loves you . . . now and forever

Dinner with Mommy

"Hey Ma hi you" that was the first thing I said to her then Gay told me that Mommy cooked Italian Spaghetti to day at OT (in the hospital) I was tied and needed a bath hadn't planed not to stay long but when I saw that Mommy had put everything she had into fixing this Spaghetti I washed my hands seat right in front of her and got down. It seemed to be the best she had ever made, Gay had her plate to and between bites I look up and she was taking pitchers of me enjoying Mommy's food and she said just what I was thinking "this is your best ever Mommy" we looked at each other with the same look. No one could make Italian Spaghetti like Ma. I had brought her this little stuffed Mousse she fell in love with it. I went to say something to Mommy and looked at her she had the stuffed Mousse and was sound a sleep she look so sweet I held back my tears and just thanked the Lord for her and asked to heal my dear Mother I love so much. You see I don't think anyone knew how hard this is on me I wanted to give Mommy her good health back even one of my Lungs but doctors said I couldn't. So you see even in the hospital Mommy was still trying to take care of Gay and me. I am blessed with the best Mother in the world.

Love You Ma Milt

Dedicated to Mommy from Milton Hall Jr #1 Son

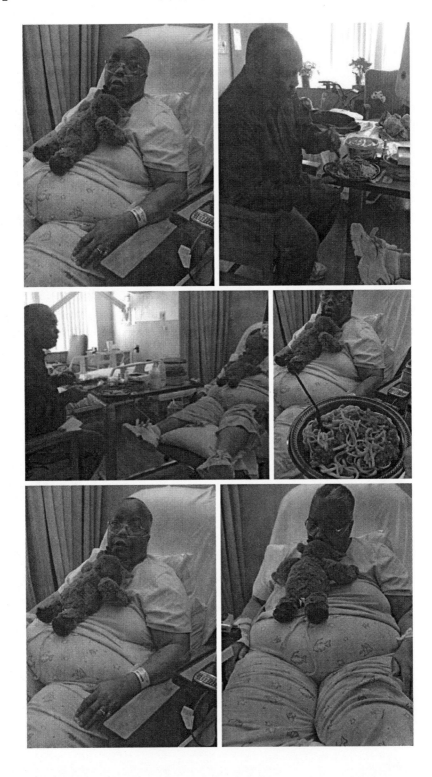

From Mama to a Son or Daughter

Mother remains your Mama
In spite of how you may feel
Love hides a multitude of faults
Tolerance breaks a strong will
Only God can make you see
The strength of Mama's love
Never in a million years
Mama's love is a Godly love
Mixed with laughter and tears
Humble yourself my son
Always remember who gives a Mama's love
Love unchangeable and steadfast
No matter how you act.
Mama's love just keeps on growing and growing.
Even when you don't love back
Just remember a Mama's love
Can only come from Mother
Rarely do you get the chance to love and enjoy another

I Wish

I wish I could not be this way
Or should I say I wish I could understand why I'm this way
Am I insecure?
Am I jealous and insecure?
Do I have a problem with something from my childhood?
I want so much to be special.
I have even prayed that I would not care that I would understand
But I find myself going backwards instead of forward.
I'll give gifts from my heart, to be accepted.
I make comments that I really mean, to be accepted
I send greetings that I truly want to send to be accepted.
Help me understand
Is family only blood
Is family part time
Am I expecting too much.
At my age I should be over this feeling
But it seems to be worse
I know God loves me
Spiritually this is wonderfully true and real
Why isn't this enough
I would like to be honest
I have always wanted to be
A total family member in every aspect
Just once
If not, why call me family

I Wonder

I wonder what happened to my grandson
Who I thought loved me so much
I wonder what's going on he doesn't stay in touch.
I wonder what happened to his tender heart
That would actually cry when I sing from my heart
He loved Blessed Assurance and Does Jesus Care
More than anything I ever sang
I wonder what happened to my number one
That would stop by to see if I had a need
Who always told me I love you Granma
Don't forget my Mac and Cheese
I wonder who or what could bring about such a change
Who makes me feel like I no longer exist
I think this is such a shame
I call you, pray for you and talk about you everyday
I look for you to just talk to me, don't treat Granma this way
If you could tell me one thing that I have done
That keeps you away no attention do you pay
I would do whatever it takes to fix this right away.
I love you so much all your life and that will never change
If you really care about me you would love Granma just the same
So since I never see or hear from you day or night
The only thing left for me to do
Is love you, sit down, and write
I pray and wonder, I wonder and this is just a part,
What does me more harm than anything else
Is how this breaks my heart
I love you always, hope life is wonderful and full of fun
You are and always will be Granma's number one
God Bless You my Grandson

If I Had My Way
If I had my way
I would hold you every day
When you were a baby dear heart
In my lap was where you would stay
Grandma's lap is what you would say
And up you would go as I lovingly rocked you to sleep
Oh how I loved that day
Even as you got older my baby
You would jump up and say Grandma's lap
For that was your favorite place to be
As you set at the Computer and read your book "Just Grandma and Me"
We are as happy as we could be, "Just Grandma and Me"
If I had my way
We would talk every day
I have so much I want to say
I would see you once in a while
Enjoy a conversation and admire your beautiful smile
If I had my way we could go out to dinner
I would have a chance to tell about times you were a winner
How you love to dance around the house
How I enjoyed that, you made me smile
You taught me a song no weapon formed against me shall prosper
If was given a chance I would ask you how you are getting along
How you are doing in college and how to stay strong
Since I can't do any of these things
They all seem to have vanished in away in the shadows
What will never change is how much I love you still
No matter come what may never forget our Days
I love you more than words can say more each and every day
I wish for you God's blessings on this your very special day
All the best God brings your way and in His loving arms you stay
If I had my way we would be closer each and every day
Grandma Loves You much

My Brother-In-Law
One Who Loves Gardening
Use any name
What can I say about my brother-in-law, Robert
I didn't see him every day
But my husband James before he died
Would take me by Robert's way
Whether it was raining, sunshine, or hot
Early morning or afternoon
We would find Robert digging in the earth
Humming some little tune
We would ask Robert, "How are you doing?"
He would answer, "Oh, I feel great.
I'm trying to finish this garden before it gets too late."
I remember the times when he was in the hospital
At this time he was very sick
He would smile and say, "James, I got to get out of here
Cause I got a lot of things to fix."
It amazing how Robert loved to work in the soil
Plant seeds and watch them grow
He took great pride in his gardens
Even when some crops grew slow
After a while others would come by and talk with him
I would sit in the car and watch
Robert would dig and water and feel that dirt
It seemed like he would never stop
He would stand back and look, wipe the sweat from his brow
Then he would go and dig some more
He would say, "Hey, James, give 'em six or eight weeks
They will be ready to eat and better than what you get from the store."
Robert said, "Come look . . . I got collards, tomatoes, and string beans
I did them other folks' gardens, too
You know you ought to come and get you a spot
You can make some money for sure."
Yes, that was just one of the many things
My brother-in-law could do
I could name many, many more like hunting and fishing
Just to name a few
Sometimes we really don't know a person

We don't see their worth or notice the kind things they do
We let time slip by most times too busy or shy
To even say I love you
Now Robert cannot hear us anymore
Or see the things we do
No more can we hear him say the words
Thanks, I sure appreciate all of you
But he left us many fond memories
That we can cherish and adore
I know every time I go by the little street
Where your beautiful gardens grew
I'll always remember the beauty and kindness I saw in you
Rest in Peace Rob
Your sister-in-law

My Mama's Gone Away
No more weeping from loneliness
No more waiting night and day
No more looking for someone who does not come
My Mama's gone away
No more watching the time
No more pains and crying
No more wondering if she's in the way
Yes, you can stop worrying
There's no need hurrying
My Mama's gone away
No more giving her care, fixing her hair
Giving her meals and her medicine, too
No trying to find excuses when you know she's looking for you
Well you can ease your mind, everything's fine
My Mama's gone away
No more suffering, bent with years
Body's tired from stress and strain
No more heartaches, feeling shut out
For reasons she cannot explain
Just take a load off yourself, no more pretending this day
My Mama, she's gone away
Now when old age comes upon you
When your time has come to go
When you have to sit back and take things you don't like
Too weak to lift your voice
When your rights have been taken, your body is shaken
When you're not even given a choice
Be sure you can say
I did my best before my Mama went away
Be sure your tears are from missing her
Be sure your conscience is clear
Be sure you have done all you could do
The years that she was here
Be able before you close your eyes
You can always truthfully say
Thank God for giving me Mama to care for and love
She's at home with Him today.

No Doubt
Mona
She used to ask
Over and over again
How can Jesus love me
I haven't always been good
Or behave like I should
Yet He loves me when I thought no one could
I guess I sound like a broken record
Repeating myself over and over again
Do you really, really love me Jesus
When will I know Lord, when
I have a mother who says she loves me
I have a brother and sister too
I have children, grandchildren
And lots of family
They say they love me too
I believe they do
I know this may sound foolish
But Lord what about you
I wake up crying
My body in pain
Family and friends say
Honey you'll be ok
Then I ask
But what will I do
Will all of you go away
I never thought
One day I would be leaving you
Not you leaving me
No more sorrow, suffering, grief, and pain
But eternal victory
Well, when I accepted the Lord Jesus Christ
This I know for sure
She confessed her sin
Asked Jesus into her heart
When the church opened their door
She said I gave the preacher my hand
But I gave the Lord my heart
Now I know how much Jesus loves me
And He gave me a brand new start

Our Family

There are many reasons families separate. Let me just name a few. Families separate because of: new locations, marriage, military, disagreements, illness, even death. But only

one thing brings families together. That one thing is love. Today love is shown.

Using the word "family" I will give just a small portion of this family:

F We are friendly, fabulous, and even famous and most of us know the Lord.

A After all these years one to six generations We look so good

Let's give this glory to God.

M Many have gone on home to glory. They won that final flight

I In spite of hardships, ups and downs, we are able to come and unite

L Looking out at this human rainbow Living to see us together today

laughing, lounging, and sharing stories is a beauty to behold

Y To our youth the young look around you.

We are climbing the ladder of age

Stay in touch learn from us how we are making the grade

Our lives have not been easy

We haven't reached perfection yet

But with Christ the center of our lives

Our future will be meaningful, full of love and respect . . .

When we leave each other let's remember

Family is a treasure we must hold dear

Let's stay in touch, it doesn't take much

And we hope to see you all next year

Our Doll

Our doll was the greatest doll of all
It had zippers, buttons and much, much more
Come on now, let's open the door
Ten little fingers
Ten little toes
One little mouth
One little nose
Two little eyes
Shining bright
Open and close the zipper
Oh, boy, that's fun
This doll was full of surprises
We were always amazed
To see all the things our doll could do
When we've got a cold and don't feel good
This doll would make our frown a smile
Ten little fingers
Ten little toes pointing down
A red little nose
Two eyes teary and stained
Open the window
And guess what we see
The little birdie looking at me
One little button
Goodness little nose
Two shiny little eyes watching, to see if it grows
Underneath a blue shirt and a string
Lace it up over and over again
A red little necktie with a hole
That is where the little button goes
Little striped pants red blue and yellow
Purple, white and green
It's so pretty and so clean
Two little red feet
To match his hair
Little left foot has a snap
Hiding under there
Little right foot has numbers

One two three four five
And my little doll is soft and cuddly
And very soft inside
I wonder if my doll can do any tricks
I'll ask my brother, it used to be his
My brother will soon be age six
You see my Grandma bought it
My Mommy and Auntie love it
My Daddy washed it squeaky clean
But it's my brother I thank most of all
Because he handed it down to me
I'm so happy
They kept it around
Tucked away safe and sound
What's his name
Oh, I thought you knew
Why his name is Happy Clown

Our Grandma

We sure will miss you Grandma
Your encouragement, your help, your smile
Our conversations we had on the telephone
When we didn't see each other for a while
We'll miss your wonderful letters
You always knew what to say
Whether we agreed or disagreed
Sometimes we would talk about
What you told us
Way into the night
Then we all would soon discover
Our Grandma told us right
Grandma you wasn't afraid to tell us
How to face life's ups and downs
When it came to telling us
We did wrong
You did not play around
And oh, Grandma, how we enjoyed
The delicious foods you cooked
We wished we had encouraged you
To have your very own cookbook
The biscuits, rolls, pies, and cakes
Preserves and chicken, too.
Whether you fixed them at home
Or sent them by mail
No one could do it quite like you
Grandma you cannot hear us
But we'll say just how we feel
It will never, never be the same
Knowing that you are not here
But we know that death
Comes to us all
We know not how or when
Yet we also know that one day, Grandma, we will see you again

The Joy of Moms & Grandmas

When God made moms and grandmas
He made them very strong
Even when their body grows weak
He adds strength to their legs and arms
Feet and legs to run to them
Arms to hug and gently squeeze their side
Whenever there's a need
Oh what joy to have that strength from God
Sons and daughters
Grandsons and granddaughters too
It brings so much joy you can even adopt a few

Thinking of You
Mom
My son . . . my son
What have you done
Why nothing Mom . . . said he
I was just out thinking
And I thought about you
Well . . . this is just something I wanted to do
Give you this gift from me to you
What is the occasion
Is this a celebration
That perhaps I overlooked
No Mom it's not
This is to show I haven't forgot you
To show you how much my Mom means to me

To The Family

The family circle has been broken
A precious link is gone from the chain
Her earthly life is over
But eternal life she gained
It's sometimes so hard to accept
That death just has to be
We know there is a reason
Beyond our power to see
Now her earthly life book is closed
But the memories we hold still dwell
Her smile, her kind deeds and humor
Are what the pages tell
So, a loved one, a friend and a pal is gone
The shock is hard and severe
We never thought it was your time to leave us
We never knew death was so near
Only God and we who love you
Can ever know or tell
The agony and pain of parting
We hate to say farewell

To the Family

What a blessed event
What a sight to behold
What a celebration to be
A part of this prestigious family
This great generation I thought I'd never see
What a blessed family this is to me

What Can Grandma Do?

When I have a granddaughter that I love as much as you
And there's no conversation between us
What does Grandma do?
When I want to hear your voice saying, "Grandma, I love you"
Just a few words
Great or small
What does Grandma do?
When I ponder in my heart
What could I have done
To have my granddaughter so distant from me
Tell me what is your point of view
And what can Grandma do?
I search my heart and my mind
Even my very soul
I ask what could I have done to you
I always pray and I ask the Lord
What can Grandma do?
I miss you, my granddaughter, so very much
I miss your voice, your smile, our conversation, and a hug
I'm asking you like I ask the Lord
What can Grandma do?
I always ask when there is pain
Search yourself, then do your part
To find a reason or a cause
Never let it go unnoticed
Don't break another's heart
Do you know what this is doing to Grandma
Each and every day
Not speaking, having nothing to do with me
It's eating my heart away
What can Grandma do?
Ask me, tell me, show me
Explain to me if you can
I deserve to know the reason
What on earth has gone wrong
Please tell me, what can Grandma do?
No one else knows better except the Lord
No one knows better than you
I'm waiting and hoping that you and only you
Tell Grandma what to do

You and Your Mother
Notice the title of the poem
It's you and your Mother.
Not our Mother or the family Mother
But you and your Mother.
I wasn't brought up with a Daddy
He died soon after I was born.
So all I remember is Mother
It was God and her alone
Sometimes we let the welfare do
The things that you could do
You may say there are other children
That may very well be true
But I'm not asking the family
I'm asking about your Mother and you.
Whether she be young or old
With pain she brought you here
After carrying you in her womb 9 months
Think of the suffering she went through.
You can't remember your infancy
Some things in your childhood you've forgotten
But with God's help she raised you

GET WELL

May the Lord heal your mind, body, and spirit as you go through illness.
May you be able to endure anyhow as you strive for wellness.

Get Well

Lovingly listen to Jesus
Ever earnestly endeavoring to endure
Victory will voice its vibrant power
That's what God has promised you
Every time God tunes your
Ears to hear
Every time He speaks He knows
Real soon you will hear
The reverence of His good news
I am standing right here
Never intending to leave you
Nor let you suffer more than you can bear
Lift up your head my child
Don't you think of losing your smile
For I knew before you were conceived
You would have your share of trials
But you have no need to worry
Remember . . . if I could not take care of you
I would never have brought you here
God loves you and so do I

Get Well Soon (God's Flower Garden)
Dear one
Get well soon
Remember the garden
God calls His own
And the beautiful flowers there
He plants them nourishes them
And keeps them in His care
Then God sees one of His flowers
More special than all the rest
He plucks it and places it
Where He can use it best
Wherever He places His flower
It still blooms and spreads and grows
It passes on to other flowers
Whenever God tells it so
His flowers never die
His flowers never fade away
God puts another flower in that place
To pluck another day
Oh what a beautiful garden
God has all colors, size, and hues
It's good to know
That in God's garden
Those flowers are me and you
We never know where God can use us
We never know just when
We never know when He will pick us out
To serve or a soul to win
We must grow in love and patience
With kindness
Bright and fair
Then God can use us
As His beautiful flowers
Anytime and anywhere
Thank God for placing you in my life (Two Beautiful Flowers)

INSPIRATION

My Vitamins

These are words from the Lord through me to give you the inspiration you need to get through the struggles of your life.

Asleep

Asleep, asleep blessed asleep to weep
A calm and undisturbed repose
Unbroken by the last of foes
O how sweet
To be for such a slumber meet
What hope and confidence it brings
To know death has lost its vicious sting
My heart is filled with sorrow for my loved one is gone
Remembering, caring and sharing the moments that we talked alone
When affliction presses the soul
Like a weight the troubles roll
That friend's name is Jesus
He is the one

A Card for You
This is a Card from the Lord

On your birthday I ask the Lord what can I or where can I get a card for the man of God for his birthday. So as always the Lord gives me what I ask for, when and how he wants to. He first reminded me of my mother, when I was a child. Mama did canning when she canned fruit after she picked & washed the fruit she cooked the fruit and put it in the jars. She would pour wax on top when the wax cool, it would harden. So I asked Mama why do you pour wax on the fruit? Mama said the wax keeps the fruit fresh and it preserves the fruit. The longer the fruit is in the jars the better it taste, it stays fresh and no mold gets to if and it last for years. Now I said to the Lord, how can I use this in the card. Well the Lord showed me this. Bishop now that the Lord has blessed you to see another year, a year you have not seen before you had a natural birthday and you may feel, Oh I'm getting older nor my physical body is not as strong as it used to be. I have artificial legs, my hands grew not as agile as they used to be, there are several things going on, I feel I'm not or won't be able to do the things I want to do for the Lord. I'm dealing with some things that only God and I know about.

Bishop, the Lord said this is true you are human, you are limited. It's normal to have these concerns, but remember the Lord gives you power to the faint, and when you get tired and worn out I the Lord offers strength, when you are exhausted and feel like you can't go on. The Lord will give you new strength. Bishop you have two birthdays you know this spiritual birthday is the one that will bring you a new revelation everyday. You see God has preserved you. Sanctified you filled you with the Holy Ghost and fire. Think about it this way. Like Mama's preserves. First you are the fruit you were picked by God 2nd you had to be washed in his blood cleanse. 3rd You had to be cooked, go thru the fire endure some physical and spiritual hardships. 4th God put some ingredients into in your preserve you. He put gifts and talent in you. 5th Then the fire had to be applied in order for you to last thru it all. 6th The wax is your faith. You know by Grace you are saved thru Faith. This is the wax that seals and keeps you with that fresh anointing as long as you process these things. The Lord will be to you the preserve. The longer you live the better he will be to you in you. He will let you feel, not see but feel new legs, that will have you leaping, dancing, running as never before.

He has a way of banishing pain. While you are praying for healing to others, God will heal you. While you are pleading the blood of Jesus to cover someone else his blood will cover you. You know how that wax on the preserve keep it for years. That spiritual seal, the Lord Jesus Go Holy

Spirit will keep you not for years but forever. No weapon formed against will prosper, you are not going anywhere until the work God has begun in you is finished. The Lord said "Wait on him, that is wait and weight cast it all on him. Trust in him with all your heart, Be strong in the Lord, let him continue to order your steps, be that light unto pathway. Whatever God tell you to do, don't be afraid, don't hesitate, step out on faith and don't look at anything or anyone. Look only to Jesus. You know Peter walked the water he was doing the impossible as long as he kept his eyes on Jesus. When he looked down he began to sink. The Lord gave me this song for both your birthdays. 1. Guide Me O Thou Great Jehovah Pilgrim through this barren land. I am weak, but thou art mighty hold me with thy powerful hand bread of heaven, feed me till I want no more bread of heaven feed me fill I want no more. 2. Open now the crystal fountain whence the healing water flow let the fiery cloud pillars. Lead me all my journey through strong deliverer, be thou still my strength & shield. Strong deliverer be thou still my strength & shield. 3. When I tread the verge of Jordan bid my anxious fears subside, bear me this the swelling current lane me safe on Canaan's side songs of praises I will ever give to thee. Songs of praises I will ever give to thee. Have a Blessed, Blessed Birthday. The Best Birthday of All Was When You Gave Your Heart to God and He Gave you new Life. Thank you Lord.

A Special Daughter with Special Needs

From Mommy to my Baby Gaynell

Lord I thank you for my daughter my special little girl the cutest little thing you could ever want to see Gaynell weighed two pounds 3 ounces at birth had no hair eyebrows toenails fingernails eyelashes eyebrows just one smooth little angel she was a fighter from the first day of her life I feel so blessed to have her in my life she calls me mommy and I call her my baby I am honored to have my baby she has never given me any trouble is not hard to deal with and is always here when I need her and she'll give me anything my heart desires Gaynell is known as my shadow always right under my feet I never had to search hard to find her she is always at my beckon call I feel like the luckiest mother in the world though many don't understand what kind of relationship we have at hand God knows just what we had need of so he put a special daughter with special needs right in my hands as my baby would always say the Lord knew that through every thing she would go through child abuse the years of damage to her mind body and spirit as well as her mental abilities were severely damaged this abuse sent my child through torture torment and severe mental anguish and illness after enduring all of its she was injured by a drunk driver and now lives a life in a wheelchair no longer able to stand walk run away she loved to her injuries were severe her closed head injury sent her back to special education for the second time the first time from the child abuse this time from the injury so in addition to the normal childhood teenage young adults and even adult every day issues one has to deal with Gaynell's was much harder for her to get through so the Lord knew He would have to prepare me to be the kind of Mommy that she would need I'm so thankful be able to be the kind of mother that a special child like mine would need but I give all the credit to the Lord for He is the one that prepared me for a long and difficult road my daughter went half the Lord taught me through His word how to best teach nurture bond with and love my daughter what a blessing to have a special daughter with special needs she has truly blessed my life Gaynell Mommy loves you

From Gaynell to my Mommy

Thank you Lord the perfect gift a special Mommy designed with me in mind for a special daughter with special needs. You see growing up a child with special needs God knew I would need a Mommy just like you. Mommy you were designed with me in mind by God because he knew how I would be. So hopefully this will help all to understand why you Mommy mean so much to me the bond we have is so special that is difficult for others to understand or to see but I will hold on to all you gave me I am grateful to the Lord for blessing me with a Special Mommy just for me.

Be Patient

Hurry up and end the service
I've got to eat
Jesus went 40 days without food
Was tempted by the devil to turn stone to bread
Our Lord still didn't retreat
We may say that's Jesus
He was perfect I just can't take it like He did
Yes, He was perfect, blameless that's true
Be patient when in service
Be glad that you could come
Everything you planned can wait
It will be there when you go home

Bishop

I prayed, I asked the Lord to give me what to say show me what they
meant. He gave me these words. In your dreams and visions was this.
In dollars in your dreams years ago was your belief. If I had the money
(dollars) I could do so much for the Lord. I would be able to build this and
that for my people. Before you were born Bishop, God had already chose
you to rescue and lead his people. Bring souls to him as you grew in the
Lord your dreams became visions.

God began to show you the dollars, the pennies, the silver, the pecans
even the green grass all these things meant something spiritually and
physically. God said you continue to do, what I ordained you to do, what I
called you to do, rescue my people.

God said: They will come with pennies (very little poor)

They will come with dollars (rich)

They will come with silver (great gifts)

They will come with pecans (food)

These represent an abundance of material things

No matter how they come (rescue them) all souls are mine

God said I will give you, whatever you need; everywhere you go I will
provide for you.

You will have money (piles as you saw the piles of dollars)

Food and gifts of all kinds your life in the ministry will be like green
grass (pastures) fresh with spiritual dew. You didn't see dirt, mud or rocks
in your dreams, you didn't see brown dead grass or stubble you saw green
grass (He maketh me to lie down in green pastures)

God showed you silver, you know silver represents riches. God is showing
you riches in glory, wisdom, and strength. He's showing you blessings
immeasurable. These are spiritual and material things you will receive.
Bishop you will never fully know why God chose you God will let others
see and God will lead others to you to tell you how they see God working
in you and thru you. You will be praying and busy bringing others to the
Lord giving them the plan of salvation. Praying for the sick and shut
in and shut out, praying and caring for the weak. Preaching and telling
the word. Every time you give God will multiply and give back to you.
Bishop the Holy Spirit is speaking faster than I can write. God said as
long as you follow Him keep doing what He called you to do rescue His
people. You will daily see His rewards spiritual attributes and more. He
said don't focus on what you want He already knows. Just stay focused on
what he wants you to do.

Continue to listen to the leading of His Holy Spirit
Bishop remember the green grass-God's grace is as plentiful as the blades
of grass and fresh as the dew that falls on it.
Dollars-Deliverance-doubled over the Devil can't stop it don't doubt about it.
Silver-Salvation, more precious than silver or gold and security
guaranteed Pennies-Prayer and privilege knowing you can take everything
to God.
Pecans-Food promises for your body and your soul.
These are just a few benefits God has in store for you. Keep on reaping
the harvest God promises you Bishop. You haven't seen a glimpse of what
God has for you.

Black People Black Heritage
Listen to me people
People of color . . . people young and old
Listen to the story
That for centuries has been told
They talked, sang, prayed and marched
For freedom every day
Their nights were spent scheming and planning
How to keep prejudice and hatred away
Oh there are so many black people
Who left legacies great and small
They left footprints in the sand of history
I could never name them all
Black heritage is what these men and women
Handed down from past generations
Many lost their lives
Because of their color and beliefs
They came from many nations
When I read of them then
I think of now
What can I leave
When I am gone
How can I bequeath so great a heritage
As these black people show
I thought of how we can have our place in history
We can look up references
Read from our books
Search for our roots like Alex Halley
These black people we read and talk about
Worked extremely hard
And what many of us may not know
They believed in the Almighty God
Why there was Simon of Cyrene
Who carried Jesus' cross
And King David's Grandmother Ruth
There was Moses' wife Zipporah
And the brilliant Dr. Charles Drew
The Queen of Sheba
Rehab of Jericho

And Enunch the Ethiopian
These are just a few in Biblical times
Who yet live in our devotions
I mentioned before how we too can leave
A page in history
How each of us young and old
Can have a P.H.D.
Using the words "Black Heritage" can help me explain how we as blacks can
live and die leaving a heritage of dignity not shame

B Be the best that you can be
L Love the Lord with all your heart
A Ask what you will, believing you will receive an answer.
C Choose a role model with Christian character
K Kick the habit of saying "I can't"

H Hear and believe the Gospel.
E Do not envy.
R Reach for excellence.
I Insist on giving your all
T Tell others "Jesus Saves"
A Always strive to be a good example
G Remember God . . . guidance goes before you whenever you ask Him.
E Everyone will tell you how but only God can show you how.
So, you see, Black Heritage is worthwhile
It's important to you and me

P for praise and practice
H for hearing and helping
D for deliverance and doing
Earn your P.H.D. by being faithful to God and to your church and to your
fellow man. Do not get your P.H.D. from Street University.
Point out to black children, men, and women that they are not merely
descendants of slaves, but sons of kings and queens
Let the color black give race a proper perspective
Let your race be a people with statements of faith for the future

Boy Child-Man Child

T - Tyrone, son of Ed and Chris
    I have known you since you were a child
Y - You used to deliver my paper
    I still remember your smile
R - Raised by parents who love you and always taught you to do right
O - Only God in all His wisdom knew one day you would carry His light
N - Now you are a grown man
    Not knowing what God has in store
E - Each day, each night, you walk with Him
    He will encourage you and show you more
B - Bridge the gap between age and churches
A - Always put God first
R - Run the race before you with patience
T - Through trouble, trials, and tribulations
    After righteousness always thirst
E - Every day with Jesus is sweeter than the day before
    When Satan tries to hinder you
    Jesus will say Tyrone I am the door
E - Endeavor to do the will of God
    Enjoy your life with Him
    Ever trusting, ever knowing in everything you do
    God will never let you down
    Even when the way seems dark and grim
Tyrone, you are a young man
So were Timothy, David, Daniel, and Jeremiah
Just to name a few
Study about them to keep you strong
Know that God will do the same for you
I am praying for your strength man/child
For you are a child of God
I am praying that you remain steadfast
Remember the race is not given to the swift nor the strong
Remember only what you do for Christ will last
From a Spiritual Mother who loves you

Burdens

Burdens you can share
Burdens you must bear
No one knows the weight
Of your burdens
Everyone's burdens are heavy
We need someone to help us bear our burdens
There are some burdens no one can help us bear
But at least we can care
That is sharing a burden
Mental anguish
A fearful leap into the shadow alone
The burden of sin is one we cannot share or bear
Jesus Christ bears it for us
Are you carrying a burden of sin
If so let the Savior in
Then the Lord can share the burdens we bear
Because we then have the strength of Christ within

2 Chronicles 7:14

If my people who are called by My Name, shall humble themselves and pray and seek My face and turn from their wicked ways Then will I hear from heaven, and will forgive their sin, and will heal their land. If My people—all souls belong to God but this I believe are souls that have accepted Jesus Christ as a personal Savior.

Shall humble themselves-stop feeling that man is in charge, in control, can fix anything, can solve every problem and not going to God in prayer for advice. Not using the road map, the problems solver, the defender, the Peace Maker, the answer to every situation.

And pray-To the Heavenly Father that He will give us the spirit of meekness which is what we need today, we are teachable, make that road map, which is the Holy Bible-the inspired word of God. Use it as our guide in making decisions in every walk of life.

And seek My Face-Look to Jesus wrestle, fast, search, hold on until you see the answer.

Turn from their wicked ways—Admit we are helpless, we do not know everything, this Earth is not ours, the Earth is the Lord's and the fullness thereof, the world and they that dwell therein. Stop the hatred, stop the killings, stop the lies and stop the prejudice as mentioned before all souls are mine saith the Lord.

Then will I hear from Heaven—When we are humble, when we humbly pray when we honestly turn from our wicked ways, the Lord takes our requests, our longings, our sufferings, our tears, and our pains, presents them to the Father God does not turn anything away from His son Jesus because He, Jesus, dies for every sin-past, present and future. He will answer in His own Way, His only way, the right way.

And will forgive their Sins-Every prayer is heard, every prayer is answered, every prayer is accepted, every one He, Jesus, says, "Yes, no, or wait". The sinner's prayer is heard when they repent. The Righteous Prayer is heard and availeth much. The Waiteth Prayer is answered and they shall renew their strength.

And will heal their land—Now do we see how merciful, how kind, how compassionate-how gracious, how great, how powerful, how awesome God is? God and God alone can and will heal our land that belongs to Him, He loaned it to us because He loves us. He blesses us every day, even those of us that don't love Him, don't serve Him, don't believe in Him, He sends the rain, sunshine, on the just and unjust. He allows us to prosper, even when satan tries to rule us, to deceive us, to lead us into traps and has no way out for us. He, God, is the way in and the way out. When we see no way, God and God alone makes a way out of no way. But the most precious thing of all even after He gave His only Son, Jesus, to die for your sin, my sin, the sin of the whole world. He loves us so much, He, God, is always right there willing and waiting to heal us, heart, body and soul. To heal our land that He loaned us, to use until we leave this Earth.

Think about it. God created all of us in His image, His Likeness then gave His only Begotten Son. He, God, loves, God heals and God forgives.

Praise Be To God, Praise Be To His Son Jesus

Praise Be To God's Holy Spirit

Complaints

Complaints, complaints, complaints
We just don't understand
Have we forgotten that Jesus was on this earth
As God, as the Son, yet man
He was ridiculed, jeered at, and spat upon
He was human just like you and me
Complaints, complaints, complaints
Are we blind? Why can't we see?
Wake up O ye Christians
I'm talking about you and I
The master of the universe was perfect
He suffered for you and I
He was not murdered or killed
As some may think
As if He had no choice
He could have sent ten thousand angels
To have the whole wide world destroyed
So here we are complaining.
Hurry up and end the service
I'm hungry, I've got to eat
Jesus went 40 days without food or water
Was tempted yet he didn't retreat.
We may say that's Jesus. He was perfect
I just cannot take it the way He did
Yes, He was perfect, blameless that's true
But he never once used His omnipotent power
He suffered for me and you
As a human being, yes a flesh and blood man
So today in Him we can stand.
When we have a headache
Think of the crown of thorns around His head
When we think of Jesus and how He suffered
For you and me on this earth
Our complaints will be gone.
When we look on this body as temporary
Think of our new body, our new home
Every inch of His body suffered
No part of our Lord escaped the pains

Let's stop complaining, keep praying
By faith we can sustain
His hands and feet were nailed
Thorns around His head
They broke His bones, they pierced His side
To be sure our Lord was dead
He drank the bitter cup alone
He spoke these words
"Father forgive them for they know not what they do."
How about it Christians
Ready to be thankful and grateful
Instead of complaining
I certainly do, don't you?

Faith and Hope

I may never be rich or famous
I may not succeed or fulfill all my dreams
I may not have many pleasures nor use my talents without measure
I may never make the headlines or even make TV
I may not ever make it around the world
Most people may never notice me
No one may ever buy my poems or forgive me for my wrongs
Nor help me with my weaknesses or tell me I'll be strong
Many may see me fake a smile but never see me cry
Some may never visit me not until I die
Yet I shall remain happy
My faith and hope remain unscathed
Because I know with assurance
Every good thing I desire
Will be given by the almighty God
He knew me even before my birth
He knew what I would have on this earth
Since my sins He has forgiven
He has for me a mansion in Heaven
So I found out without a doubt
There is no need to fear
I will receive all the good things in life
Either here or over there

Hurdles
I see my life as that of a hurdler
For example you see hurdle jumpers
They don't walk up to a hurdle
They run and run fast
They continue to run and jump
And they must jump high or they will trip and fall
At the end, when they jump the last hurdle
There's a prize or trophy waiting for them
Every day I am faced with a hurdle to overcome
I praise God because He takes me over each one
One hurdle at a time
You see praising God gives me strength to run
Singing His praises allows me to jump and run
And not just jump . . . but jump high
When I go to His house of worship
And hear my Pastor Prentice preach the word
God increases my running and jumping
The word speeds me up
Get me in a hurry
Then I just lift Him up
I know the running and jumping the hurdles in life
Will one day be over
And I too will get a prize
In fact I will receive more than one
I will have eternal life, a crown of life, and a mansion
My race will be finished
And I'll rejoice with my Lord
Of course the running and jumping is spiritual
Whatever your hurdle is
Whenever you find yourself and I know every one of us do have hurdles to overcome
Whatever your hurdles are
Seek the Lord while you have a chance
He will give you everything you need to get over your hurdles
Not only to get over them but to finish your race
And at the end you too will win a prize of prizes
Eternal life

It Was His Love

It was His love
That sent Him here
It was His love
That said the prayer
Father . . . forgive them
They know not what they do
It was His prayer that said
I offer myself for you
He took my sin
Upon the cross
He took my sin
For I was lost
It was my Savior's tender mercy
That satisfied my soul
He said my son
Rise up and let me see
The beauty I gave so freely
As my Father gave me

Jesus' Blood

All for love
His blood a ransom snatched
The sinner's soul from the grave
Jesus' blood on Calvary's Mountain
All who would believe can be saved
Could there ever be a price placed on anyone to pay
Would you give your life as He did
What would be your answer today
He alone the price did pay everything
He gave a way
Left no cause for any to stray
The righteous one, the mighty one
The perfect Lord and Christ
Suffered bled and died
For all He rose
He lives to give us life

Jesus Changed Me

I am no longer depraved
Because I am saved from misery and strife
As I look back on my life I ask myself
Am I the same
Am I growing in grace
Have I changed
Is there spiritual growth
Is Jesus seen in me
Has He made a difference
Can others see
Have I changed my walk
Is my conversation holy when I talk
Do I love and respect others
Do I share the good news of Jesus with my sisters and brothers
Do I cherish the cross
Minister to the lost
Pray daily some soul to win
Tell them God loves and will save them from sin
I'm still striving
Thanks be to God I'm thriving
I'm letting the light of Jesus shine
Everyday I praise and thank Him
This I know
I am not what I used to be and I can joyfully say
He's mine

Jesus Speaks

When blue skies seem cloudy and gray
I lift up my eyes to pray
Sometimes not knowing what to say
Jesus speaks to me
I listen to His voice
He has given me a choice
Hear me or not
Jesus speaks to me
How long will you carry this cloud
Come to me
Your cares unfold
Jesus speaks to me
The Holy Spirit wants to comfort you
Don't let pride take control
Jesus speaks to me
So I answered finally
Have thine own way Lord
Have thine own way
I give myself to you
Now I can freely pray.

Keep This Man
Dependable, trustworthy, honest with never ending love
Has done more for me since I met Him
Than the numbers in the sea of sand
Right or wrong . . . He's always there
I think I'll keep this man
Crazy about Him, can't live without Him
He gives with no strings attached
Available twenty-four seven
On promises He's never slacked
My favorite fan in all the land
Oh yes . . . I'll keep this man
He never fusses or grumbles
When I call Him . . . He doesn't complain
Day or night . . . He's never up tight
When I'm down . . . He's my pep pill
His embrace is always a comfort
When I'm restless . . . He whispers . . . Be still
He says don't be upset, I understand
Now you know . . . I must keep this man
If you know or have a man like this
You must know what I mean
If you have any doubts about this man I write about
Don't take my word . . . check Him out
Then tell me if you can
Wouldn't you keep such a man
If not, I'll tell you what
Do it as quick as you can
Go and get or better yet
Hold on to this man
I guess you thought I forgot
Or maybe you thought I was ashamed
To share this man or even give you His name
Everybody ought to know throughout the land
Jesus is the man

Know That We Are Blessed
Look at you vesting in your glory
Everything going your way
Everything you touch seems to turn to gold
Perhaps this could be me some day
No I don't want to be you
I don't envy what you've got
God is really good to me and he's given me a lot
Abundant grace that's truly amazing
Gives me sweet hour of prayer
Makes it well with my soul
Reminds me that He cares
Having a friend in Jesus
Who knows how much I can bear
He never lets me feel ashamed
He takes me everywhere

Let Me Share

Going to the doctor as I do often lately complaining of severe pain in my
right foot. I was saying what is this? Already seeing the doctor for other
conditions I wondered what was wrong now.

After viewing the x-ray the doctor explained this must be very painful,
but you have a degenerative joint disease. The joint in your right great
toe is gone it's deteriorated. Can you fix it I asked? He answered no it
has to be replaced. Well I was overwhelmed, but I said ok. I want to walk
without so much pain. The doctor explained you will be in a cast for
weeks and it's painful. This is when I began to talk to Jesus. I always ask
him about everything. Knowing this was a hard task that He would take
me thru. Then I began to ask Him to show me the good in this. First of
all He walks with me. He strengthens me. He shows me how I'm blessed
because I have my left foot to stand on. I have my hands to guide a walker
and wheelchair. I am limited but not totally disabled. I began to thank God
for another change, another testing of my faith. Another chance to share
with others, that no matter how rough the road, how high the mountain,
Jesus is always with us. He never takes anything away from you when
Satan attacks our bodies. God is right there to replace what we think is
gone. If it's a time in your life you are faced with an affliction you can
count and depend on Jesus. I think of the spikes that were driven thru His
feet on the cross. He wore this pain for me. I could write a book on all the
affliction the Lord has brought me through and I still could not tell them
all. On Thursday, May 9, 2006 my Pastor called. I was in so much pain I
was in tears. My Pastor Prentice prayed for me over the phone. And praise
God I haven't had a pain in my foot since. It stopped immediately. I call
this a prayer of faith. I believed and received. I know many of my sisters
and brothers in Christ can witness to healing in their life. I am sharing just
one with you. God can heal. He can deliver, He can mend our brokenness.
He has a miracle to fit your need. You just believe Him and receive.

Life Is So Precious
Life is so precious, so short, so sweet
Even ups and downs are difficult to meet
Full of emptiness . . . full of pain
Full of sunshine . . . full of rain
Full of winters bitter cold
Full of youth . . . full of old
Full of springs, autumns, and falls
Full of tragedies that affect us all
Full of mental mountains . . . full of pitfalls
Life is full of solutions . . . full of problems to solve
Full of heartaches in which we all are involved
So you see a small picture of life
With the bitter and the sweet
But a life with Christ is the best of all
He will keep you in perfect peace
I hope for you and your lovely wife
The best on earth and through all eternity
With Jesus' Joy

Light
Now the subject I
Present to you
Is L-I-G-H-T Light
The word has only five letters
But it is essential
Both day and night
You know the dictionary gives twenty-five meanings
On what light is and what light can do
But the Bible gives the real meaning
Let me present a few to you
That in Genesis 1:31-45
Then it tells of the natural light
The miraculous and the artificial
In the books of Judges and Acts
In First John one and seven
Tells us what we will have
If we walk in this light
Fellowship with one another
Oh let me tell you
This man is all right
It said Jesus, Jesus
Will take His blood and cleanse us
From not one, but all our sins
And this light will give us
Wisdom and guidance
Oh, and such peace
We will have within
Now the most beautiful part about this light
Is the favor from Christ it brings
In John 1:4-9
Just about sums up everything
Because these verses tell you
How this Holy Man was sent
To bear witness of this light
How all men, not one but all men might believe
And have a right to the tree of life
Now saints and friends here's
The only meaning

It's right here in His word
Jesus, I said Jesus
Is the true light
He is the true light
Remember what you have heard
Now here is a guild of light
To carry you through the day
To help you to see Jesus
To keep you from losing your way

L - Let the light of love shine out of your hearts always

I - Insist on illuminating someone's spirit through Christ every day

G - Go with the goal reminding yourself and others about the goodness of God's light

H - Help others to know the happiness Christ's light brings

T - Take time to pray that your light will ever shine for Christ no matter how small it is

Don't hide it under a bush. Let it shine that others may see your good works and glorify the Father who is in Heaven

My Testimony

I thank the Lord for being alive and for what he is to me
How he saved, sanctified and blessed my life
How he gave me the victory
Jesus came into my life one day
Gave me a mind to live for him
He put sunshine in my soul
When it was black
With clouds of sin
Oh Jesus filled me with his Holy Spirit
To comfort me even in tears
To keep from yielding to temptation
He takes away all my fears
I just thank the Lord
For the beautiful promise
Of life eternally . . .
I'm so glad, I am washed
In His blood
That He shed on Calvary

No One but Jesus
No one can touch me
Like Jesus can
No one can match
The touch of Jesus' hand
The moment Jesus' hand touches mine
I know I've been touched by God
No one can heal
Like Jesus can
No one else knows
The pain we bear
The moment we
Reach out to Him
He is always
Right there
No one removes doubt
Like Jesus can
No one can hold you
In His powerful hands
As soon as you
Reach out to Him
You know
You've been
Touched by God
He sends His angels
To watch over you
Night and day
He protects you
In every way
He finds you when
You stray
Then you know
You've been found by God
In times of trouble
In hurt and harm
He holds you in
His loving arms
He whispers . . . I am with you
In the midst of the storm
Always know
You are sheltered by God

POWER

P - Please God
O - Order My Step
W - Will You Guide Me All the Way
E - Elevate Me In
R - Renew a Right Spirit In Me

Project P.L.A.C.E.

Life is a challenge . . . many problems to face
Mistakes are often hard to erase
Mental mountains seem to reach outer space
Sometimes brings us undue disgrace
When we have disappointments as I know
Since we cannot handle them alone
Don't despair, someone cares
Let me present help for you
I'll use each letter in Project PLACE
To introduce some of the things they do
With God and the skills of others
Hope can be returned to you
P Please don't think I'm presumptuous
When I say we begin with prayer
R Reaching out to others is our strength
O Only you can keep us here
J Join in, become a part of discerning right from wrong
E Equality for all, making a better life
With arts, crafts, and songs
C Counseling, cooking, and courage taught
By people just like you
They are qualified to say, you can do it
Because, you see, we've been there, too
T Take a chance, it's a challenge
The change will do you good
P Peace that passeth all understanding
L Love unconditionally
A Adoration
C Christ filled
E Everlasting care
Get out of that rut . . . show some guts
Prove it to yourself and your neighborhood

Purity

P - Peace Purity and Paradise
I want to be faithful, fair and clean
I ask God for these virtues
So my life on earth will be blessed
U - Unity Understanding and Humble
Upholding Jesus wherever I may be
I pray He grant me these blessings
Let kindness be seen in me
R - Respect Righteousness, and Resolving
No resentment toward my fellow man
Requesting that God shower me
With love abundantly
I - Intensive, Interest, and Internal
Enclosed with the love of Christ
Active in His service
Attracting others to the Christian life
T - Truthful, Tactful, and Tangible
Believing the teachings and accepting God's word
Listening and observing
The Christian laws I've heard
Y - Yearning to do the will of God
Even in my youth
Yielding only to God's will
Taking on the yoke of truth

Questions and Answers

Should I? Must I?
Oh, how I want to. But, why can't I?
Question God
About how I feel within
Would He? Couldn't He?
Why shouldn't He answer me?
After all,
He said Ask, and it shall be given
Seek, and ye shall find
Knock,and the door will be opened
I know this is true because
It has happened to me
Many, many times
So, why should I be afraid to ask
Why not all my burdens on Jesus cast
I must stop climbing these mental mountains
I must heed the warning sign
Why not tell, the Almighty God
All that's on my mind
I'm sure God already knows
I'm sure He also cares
I know He's more than willing
To listen and to share
Knowing this is wonderful
Now I have a new way to pray
Dear God, In Jesus precious name
Answer my heart and my mind
Not just the words I say
My heart says do not be troubled
My mind says wait patiently
My lips are saying Lord I'm so tired
He answers, Don't worry
One day I'll make you free
Now, when I have a question
I won't be afraid, nor will I hesitate
I'll simply pray,
Dear Lord, let me remember
That you are always here with me
And you're never, never late

Sooner or Later

Sooner or later
You're gonna need Jesus
Sooner or later you're gonna need God
Why not take Him for your Savior
Why not let Him be your Lord
Cause sooner or later you're gonna need Jesus
Sooner or later you're gonna need God
He will save you
If you ask Him
He'll bring you out
When times are hard
Sooner or later
You're gonna need Jesus
Sooner or later you're gonna need God
You can call Him
You can trust Him
He'll be your light
When days are dark
Sooner or later you're gonna need Jesus
Sooner or later you're gonna need God
One day I sought Him
And I found Him
Now I know Him as my personal Lord and Savior

Sound the Drums

Sound the drums not just for a beat
Sound them loud retreat, retreat
Let our voices ring out
Bang, bang
Loud and hard
Raise the sound
God, oh God
March, march through the streets
Sound the name
Sound the name
Speak, speak
Time is passing
It waits for no one
Tell the good news
God the Father and Jesus His son
Tell the world everyone
He's coming back and you can't run
So we sound the drums
Let the world know
That the Lord is someday soon to come

Spiritual Food

*Like we feed our babies milk, raise them on certain baby foods so they
will be strong and grow. I was given extra food other than natural food
each and everyday. As long as I can remember I was fed music songs. The
difference was not just music and songs it was God's music God's songs.
They were and still are my daily bread. I can't ever remember a day even
in the night, wee hours in the morning, that a song wasn't in my heart and
sang from my mouth.*

*Like Timothy: When he said from a child I've known the scripture. He
was taught by his grandmother Lois and his mother Eunice. I was taught
by my mother Telsie B. Howard the Pastors and Saints of the church.*

*My mother sang to me, I sang to her. She taught me to pray and how to
believe God would answer my prayer. She told me to sing in season and
out of season. In other words sing when you are happy, sing when you are
sad. Singing makes you peaceful, singing makes you stand but be sure you
are singing God's Praises as unto the Lord.*

*As I grew in age and in Christ all the things Mama taught me began to
take on new meanings. I have a better understanding of singing God's
Praises. When you know Him, singing to His Glory is a Ministry. It is my
prayer that the songs I minister to you will lift those that know the Lord as
their personal Savior. Soften and prepare the hearts of those that have not
accepted the Lord. Come to ask what they must do to be saved. This is my
prayer and desire.*

The Containers on My Shelf

I think I'll clean my kitchen
I start with cleaning my shelf
I don't mind having help
With the rest of the house
But my kitchen I'll do myself
I have a little pantry
In a corner just to the left
I know where everything is in there
Even the containers on the shelf
Now I have my mop and my broom
A dust cloth and some spray
A pencil and pad for the list of the things
I have to put away
First I'll take out everything
Get my pantry good and clean
All the corners and the crevices
The cracks that are in between
Then I'll put everything back in order
Just the way I want it to be
Because there is no one that can do it better
At least not to suit me
I may even have to add a few things
Because my stock is getting low
And as much as I hate to admit it
Some of these things have got to go
Now let's suppose my body is the pantry
And my heart the containers on the shelf
Jesus can clean up my heart
The rest I'll have to do myself
First I have to clean up my body
Get unrighteousness out of my heart
Not to tuck it away until later
It must completely be destroyed
I must check and clean this body
Each and every day
I'll need a strong detergent
To keep temptations at bay
I'll let my detergent be Jesus

He is the Son of God
I'll combine Him with the Holy Spirit
To remove the stain of sin is hard
The mop I use will be salvation
Spray every corner
With His power from above
Seal every crack and crevice
With His gripping and adhesive love
I will clean every one of my containers
And every inch of myself
With the precious blood of Jesus
That was shed for me in His death
My containers must be labeled with righteousness
My shelves labeled with truth
My body must have that radiant light
Oh I have a lifetime job to do
What do I see in some containers
No this cannot be
Disobedient, slow, envy
These containers can't belong to me
There's more but no one is watching
I wonder if this just might work
Maybe I can change the labels
By giving money to charities and Church
I cannot throw away all my containers
Especially the ones carrying looks
How would I know when to roll my eyes
Turn on a smile, like a jerk
When someone is being hurt
Here is my container I've had for years
It's filled to the very top
It's my container full of temper
I have to use it quite a lot
I think I'll just hide these containers
So no one else can see
I won't use them unless I have to
No one cleans in here but me
Well here's a container all covered with dust
It hasn't been used for quite awhile

Let me clean it off so I can see
Why it's my container full of smiles
There are instructions on this container
It reads:
Delicious when served this way
One cup of truth
One cup of love used 24 hours a day
This takes away the nasty temper
The mean looks and deceit
The things that always upset us
The taste is naturally sweet
Go every minute of every day
Let this be our story
We can live and do God's will
If we take a daily inventory

The Door Is Open
An Invitation
Standing on His promises
He gives a very special grace
In the time of trouble
He is right there waiting in place
The door of the church is open
I can almost see His face
He's standing at the door of your heart
And the door of the church is open
Why not let Jesus in
He's waiting just give Jesus your heart
Just give the preacher your hand
Come on in, come on in
And be born again

The Occasion
An occasion is an opportunity. So each time I have an occasion or opportunity to:
Speak for Jesus
I feel good
Whenever I have an occasion
To give back to the Lord
I feel good
Whenever I have an occasion
To encourage someone
I feel good
Whenever I have an occasion
To hug a child or bring a smile
I feel good
Whenever I have an occasion
To sing God praises
I feel good
Whenever I have an occasion
To bear witness to someone
About the Lord and His goodness
I feel good
So now you can see why I'm so happy today. It is indeed a Together Occasion because we are together when we:
Pray Together
Talk Together
Sing Together
Eat Together
This occasion is special because it is focusing on families. This occasion is threefold because we have biological families, Christian families, and we are building families. What a wonderful way to convey our efforts my Church, our Church, but above all God's Church is a Church that participates in all of these endeavors.
I will share some valuable facts that will keep us growing together and building together.
We must be:
Clear minded
Self-controlled so we can pray
Love one another because love hides a multitude of faults
Offer hospitality to one another without grumbling

We must use whatever gifts and talents we have received from the Lord.
We must serve others faithfully, administering God's grace in its various forms.
When we speak, we must speak as one speaking the very words of God.
When we serve, we must serve with the strength God provides.
In all things be sure God gets the Glory. He must be praised and glorified through Jesus Christ.
Be a leader of God, serving not because we must, but because we are willing, as God wants us to be.
We must not be greedy for money or personal gain.
Be generous in giving back to God what He has given us.
Be eager to serve.
Be examples, giving God the glory.
As I said earlier, we must have facts to be a growing and building family . . . being a member of The Royal Family. I'm speaking about the Royal Family of God.
We have something special. A Variety Family Pack; let me give you an example. Have you noticed when you go to a food market and you see in big bright colors signs and labels reading:
Special Pack
Variety Pack
Family Pack
When you see this you know you have a good deal. Well the Royal Family of God has a special Variety Family Pack and good benefits. We have:
F God's Favor, His Fellowship and His Faithfulness. Oh great is His Faithfulness.
A We have His Assurance Blessed Assurance
M We have His Mercy, Comfort and Peace
I We have an Inheritance and Intercession
L We have His Love, Life, Light and Liberty
Y We have His Yoke, but it's made easy
We have burdens, but they are made light when we yield to Him.
Now how can I say and know these valuable facts? Because they come from the Book of Facts, the Holy Word of God, The Bible. And as a child of God I can boldly state the facts from experience.
For this very reason:
The church and all of us who want to continue to stay together as a loving family, a growing family, a building family, and above all a family of God, we must let this and all the occasions to come be based on and built on the facts and let us.

1. Add to our faith, goodness
2. And to goodness, knowledge
3. And to knowledge, self-control
4. And to self-control, perseverance
5. And to perseverance, Godliness
6. And to Godliness, brotherly kindness
7. And to brotherly kindness, love

For, if we possess these qualities in increasing measure, they will keep us from being ineffective and unproductive in our knowledge of our Lord Jesus Christ. The Facts, The Foundation, The Family Special Variety Pack. The occasion is for loving, growing and building families.

What Makes a Home

When you walk up on the doorsteps
Before you knock or ring the bell
Whether this house is up for rent
Or whether it's up for sale
The thing that really makes a home
Is when Jesus lives in there
Don't have Him as a guest who dwells temporarily
Let Him know this is your home too Lord
Live here with me permanently
You will be the head of my house
To guide, direct, and lead
You will be the one to supply my every need
So whenever someone enters
They will know that a man lives here
He lives in every room
I am totally in His care
He's with me through the thick and thin
He never leaves me alone
It is wonderful to have
The man named Jesus
To make my house a home

Why

I am so glad God inspired me to write
I have to pause every minute
as I ask Him to give me what to write
Short or long
if I don't depend on Him
I'll get it wrong
Why am I talking to you
God told me to
Why am I praying for you
God told me to
Why do I sing to you
God told me to
Even when I feel unloved
Why should I love you
God told me to
Why is it all left up to me
God said it's not all left up to me
What I command you to do
Is required of others too
So love, pray, care and support each other
This is a must
When we do for one another
Is what God does for us

JOURNEY THROUGH ILLNESS

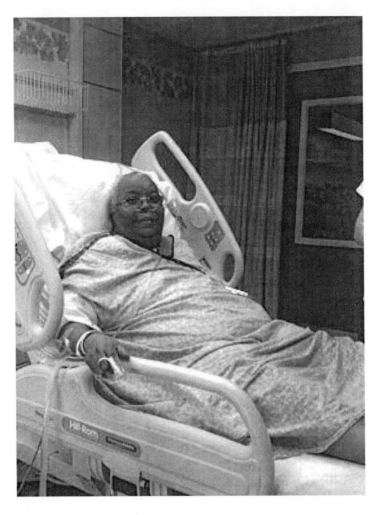

My journey through my illness at times seemed more than I could bear, but what kept me hanging on was knowing that Jesus cares. Does Jesus care? Yes, He does. So I gave it all to Him and He brought me through.

A Doctor's Visit
I saw a doctor today
He was very kind
He came to see if I was depressed
He wanted to test my mind
I really like this doctor
He said call me Dr. C
I told he was like a mirror
Through him myself I could see
He helped me to see inward
And really thinks things through
He left much too quickly
He said with a very soft voice
Good day, very nice to meet you.
With this doctor, I was very impressed
He complimented me and said you are not depressed
But if you think you ever are
Give me a call here's my card.
I want this doctor to know
In my mind he opened a door
Started me thinking about things to explore
I will surely see this Doctor C. again.
I enjoy the way he made my days begin.
Doctor C if ever I have a difficult day
In my purse I have your card
Carefully tucked away
I feel to you I can relate
From me you will get a visit
I will not hesitate
Again meeting you was a refreshing experience.

Diabetes
I am a diabetic
Don't sit around and grope
As if you have no hope
God and many others
Are here to help us cope
Don't neglect your body
Ask for the help you need to feel complete
Be a determined diabetic
Our health problems can be beat
Through healthy eating, medication and exercise
This can keep us going
Keeping your appointments, reading and learning
Being educated it's all in knowing
So rest, relax and do not be stressful
This will help get us through each day
Stand up to diabetes and you will feel better along the way
Keep the faith and say
We can live with diabetes and more
No matter come what may
There is no cure so they say
But rest assured you can live a wonderful life with it anyhow

Pain

I can understand the pain
But why does it hurt so much
It's something I can't touch
Pain you never go away
You are constantly interfering
Even when I pray
Do you intend to stay
I speak of you as if you are a person
Well I am the person you are in
Should I endure you
I can't get rid of you
You really get under my skin
I write about you
Because I can't fight you
You always seem to win
Everyday I just grin and bear it
Then start all over again
You I think I understand you pain
They told me what I have
What I don't understand
Is how you hurt so bad
Pain is like my whole body is being stabbed
Pain you've been so long with me
Should you be called a friend
Like a friend you never forsake me
And you've been everywhere I've been
Pain you're one that sticks close
You're here morning, noon and night
You don't slight any parts of my body
I never have to look for you
You just hurt from left to right
You are stubborn arrogant
You are tough as you can be
You are generous and I just found out
You are with more people than me
You are sneaky and deceitful
No one can see you in action
No matter what I take it may cover

You for a little while
Then here you are, right there in a fraction
You work hard trying to break me
This I truly know
There's not a chance
Take your last dance
I'll be here to see you
Do your last show

KIDS/YOUTH

A message to our kids and youth. They need to know and learn how much they mean to us each day. Through them learning to love, honor, respect and obey they will be blessed each and every day.

ABCs for Kids

A is for all the things I like especially airplanes

B is for boats, bears, and bubble gum shaped like choo-choo trains

C is for cows and chocolate and cannons and cotton candy WOW

D is Darth Vader and dragons, dill pickles and Danish cows

E is Easter eggs, elephants and engines roaring loud
     Eagles, ears and erasers coming out of the clouds

F is for funny books, franks, fathers and fairy tales

G is for gumdrops, Goofy, green lights and Granny's pies for sale

H is for horses, hamsters and happy days

I is for icicles, ice tea and ice cream fixed a thousand ways

J is for jump suits, jumping rope

K is for kites, Kellogg's Corn Flakes, King Kong ape and kids kicking and
     saying no to dope

L is for little boys and girls, love bugs and living on the moon

M is for Mom, money, movies, marshmallows and coconut macaroons

N is for Nutty Buddies, Now or Later and nifty cute baboons
     Nuts and raisins, nails and newspapers together in one room

O is for Orioles, oranges, octopus and Oodles of Noodles, too

P is for pushups, policemen, pillows and poodles with pots and pans to boot

Q is for questions-What is a quail

R is for rabbits, roller skates, rivers and red pears

S is for streets, sweets, sugar and spice

T is for Mr. T, talking, telling tattle tales, twinkling stars and twice

U is for uncle, umbrella, and understanding unicorns

V is for victory, video, vinegar and vines

W is for westerns like Wyatt Earp, John Wayne and wine

X is for the Xs in my soup

Y is for yogurt and all the youngsters in my group

Z is for zoos, zebras, and zucchini soup

Do you like my ABCs

Tell me, tell me, tell me, please

Choose

It's hard to be a thug or bully
You have to practice everyday,
You have to pretend you are the worst of all
You choose the wrong never the right
You have to think of nasty things to say
You have to compete with other bullies and thugs
You have to learn how to steal, rob and kill
Act like the worst in the hood to show that you are for real
You can never show respect
You cannot be seen acting nice
You sleep with weapons and nightmares
You have to get beat up once or twice
You sneak in and out so you can't be seen
You lie and scheme about everything
You get hooked up with a gang
You call them family and friends
It's hard to get out yet you fight to get in
Choose to be what God made you to be
Sin makes it hard for you to hear because you think you can't win
You weren't born this way
It's the way you choose
You are blind to what you can be
You are sure to lose
So my sons and my daughters choose to do the right thing

For Kids of All Ages
Write about any and everything
Shoes, old boots, even rings
If I don't like what I write
I just tear it up
Think some more then write about cups
Write about pickles and how to make them
Write about cookies and how to shape them
Write about things to love and things to hate
Or write about chipmunks
And someone to date
Write a song or poem
A sugar cane, a puppy
Something funny or something yucky
But use your creative minds
And just continue to write, write, write

Gone

Gone so soon
You are gone
Oh, you haven't been here long
Went so quick, left so young, gone
How and what was your experience in life
Mostly good, too much bad
Did you have a relationship with Mom and Dad
So sorry you're gone, gone, gone
Did you have a choice
When you hung your head or lifted your voice
Did we hear or know you were there
Gone, with great remorse
Gone, good-bye
Help us understand
If you could return
What would we demand
Would we just sit back and watch
Or take a stand
It's too late, you're gone
Gone in death, or to a prison
Who's to blame, who's forgiven
Would you listen and take the way out
When the chance is given
What scorn you're gone
Oh, God, Dear God, what can we do
How can we live
Happy, honest and true
Where is our shelter, who do we go to
Now that our friend is gone
We are helpless, young and frail
Nothing hurts more, we are living on the edge
We don't want to end up dead
Not at least until we lived
A productive life with something positive to give,
We are not bad, we're just scared
We are daughters and we are sons
Please don't let the streets consume us
Please help before we are all gone . . . .
Please don't let the world forsake us
Please don't let us all be gone, gone, gone

Kid's Gross Yuk
I looked at it
It was rather cute
Lots of colors
Lots of shine
And what made it really neat
The cake . . . and it is all mine
The eyes were like
Black jelly beans
Or maybe two big grapes
I was trying to chase

Short and Sweet
For Kids
Porky Pine
Porky Pine
Will you be mine
Will you stick with me
To the end
Just because you're sticky
Doesn't mean you can't be my friend
You could be my back scratcher
Your bristles will be my brush
You could help me clean my pots and pans
You could protect me when someone gets rough
Porkie Pine
Porkie Pine
I'm glad you're mine
Everyone doesn't have a friend
Who sticks with them through thick and thin

Terrific Kids

Rap with a positive message
Are you ready kids
To be happy and free
Get on your feet
Repeat after me
I wanna be a positive terrific kid
O yeah I say I wanna be a positive terrific kid
Now clap your hands
Wave them in the air
Say . . . I'm a terrific kid
And I do care
We are gonna be
Terrific positive kids
Oh yeah
We are gonna be terrific middle school kids
Now clap your hands
No need to repeat
Just listen to me and keep the beat
Come on kids I know you can do it
All you gotta do is put your minds to it
I know you can be terrific
Just keep the faith and be specific
Don't worry about trying
To be bad and cool
Made up your minds to stay in school
Your grades will get the highest bid
Remember you are terrific middle school kids
Now scream I am a terrific middle school kid

PRAYERS

Throughout every day and night I pray. I pray through song. I love to sing Gods praises. That's what takes me through my day. Trusting in the Lord with all my heart, leaning not unto my own understanding and acknowledging His way gets me through my days. So I say to you just pray.

A Broken Vessel

I'm in this place broken
Some place I don't know where
I'm knocking on an invisible door
No one else is here
Now this place is crowded, but lonely
I'm calling, can't you hear
Why doesn't someone answer
The crowd doesn't seem to care
My eyes don't see reality
My ears don't hear what I'm saying to me
Where is this place I ought to be
I'm broken a broken vessel
Oh God can you be my delivery
To the darkest, deepest silence
Where no one should want to be
Yet I'm here way out there
In the depth of misery
Give me your light
Make this blackness bright
Rescue this broken vessel please
Take these mental pieces of brokenness
Turn my frailness to strength and peace
Let this broken vessel have relief
Everyone have an empty face
There seems to be no dignity or shame
I have no pride left
I have no hope
I'm a broken vessel
With no love and no support
I sing a song that has no tune
I dance to music that has no meaning
I'm a broken vessel that just moves along
Yet standing still and being consumed
I hear voices and only one
I seem to have no exit
From the web, I've spun
The voices seem to know
Everything I've done

Now I've found comfort
I am that broken vessel
Made of earthly clay
But Jesus fixed my broken condition
And took my brokenness away

A Christmas Prayer

It may not be where or how we want it to be
But you promised us food, clothes, and shelter
That's a blessing beyond my dreams
So bless my family one by one
Lord bless them as a whole
Thank you for not letting them be hungry
And out in the cold
Help them to lift one another
In love and in gifts
Keep them together, Lord
Make your blessings swift
This is a special Merry Christmas Prayer
Sent from me to God
Please accept it from my heart
I could not go buy a card

A Prayer
Forgive the seed of discord
That I sow, whenever I speak.
For expecting others to always have pity and compassion for me
Keep mine eyes focused on Thee
Lord only you, can heal me
From the habit of misery
Complaining about what I do
How can I ever know you care Dear Lord
Unless I put my trust in you.
Lord help me to do what is pleasing to you

A Prayer for You
I pray for you
Each and every day
That God will bless
You in every way
I ask His blessings
With your health and your bills
And to give you the faith
To believe He will
And He proves He will
Hear and answer our prayer
Whenever and wherever
There is a need
He will always be there

A Request

Lord, I'm afraid
Please don't let me lose my sight
My strength, my mind
I want to live for you
Sing to you
And praise you all the time
God said don't be afraid
I have shown you what to do
The mind I gave my son, Jesus
Let His mind abide in you

Fallen

Oh Lord I have fallen
There is no hiding place
Help me Jesus . . . help me
I have fallen from Your grace
I once had a lot of money
I once had a good job
I thought that was all I needed
But now the facts I must face
All these things have vanished
Since I've fallen from Your grace

Hear our Grandsons Lord
Oh Lord hear my grandson
He's crying out to you
There are songs for mothers and fathers
Sisters and brothers too
There are cries going out for
Grandma and honors for Grandpa too
Give me an ear to hear Oh Lord
The cry from my grandson to you
We are intelligent and strong
Yet everyday we do something wrong
We strive to help and show him
Where he belongs
But he needs you dear Lord
To help him along
Hear my grandson now while he is young
Turn his steps to the path you have drawn
Show him your light and your direction
Then he will make the right connection
My grandson's cry
May be simple and short
His cries may be silent and few
Let him know Lord that it doesn't matter
Let him know he can always reach you
Dear Lord if ever a cry and a prayer is heard
Let this be the one
The cry the prayer the tears the plea
To you from my grandson

Make Me a Blessing

Make me a blessing
As I go from day to day
Counting on my own blessings
When I'm alone
Sharing them with others
Along the way
Make me a blessing
No matter how small
Whether in words or deeds
It is far better to share and care
Than to have no blessings at all
Make me a blessing
Let me not hesitate
Not waiting until I can do something great
Make me a blessing . . . don't let me wait
Make me a blessing in some way
A blessing, a blessing, a blessing today

My Prayer

Lord, you know my heart . . . my pain
Give me strength and courage to regain
The respect I lost again
Show me how not to cry
Every time a memory runs by
Inside somehow I seem to die
Help me find myself again
Don't let me be bitter
Lord, help me be strong
Help me to admit my wrong
Even if I express it in word or song
Help me find myself again

Praying For You
I grieve for you today
My spirit is heavy too
I somehow feel your burdens
There seem to be so many
They seem to be everywhere
Know that God is with you
It's not that you don't give
Your burdens over to the Lord
But you . . . like all of us are human
This makes the journey hard
I pray for you always . . .
I know you pray for me
We both know faith unlocks the door . . .
But prayer is the key

To my baby girl

Prayer Without Kneeling
I am always leaning
I don't do no kneeling
My knees are not bruised
Because they are not used
My point is this
Hear what I am saying
Don't let your knees
Stop you from praying.
Maybe you can't kneel
Because of a condition
It doesn't matter the position
God will hear, God will heal
Let your prayer be consistent
A daily routine.
Whether lying, standing, reclining or sitting
God's mercy and grace will show you pity
Don't say I can't pray because I can't kneel
If you have given your heart to Jesus
He knows how you feel
Your elbows may be bruised
Because you lean
Pray it doesn't matter, as long as your heart is pure and clean

Precious Lord Hold My Hand

Precious Lord hold my hand
As I go through life's uncertainty
Each fleeting moment rolls back into eternity
Lord hold my hand
Guide my feet O great Jehovah
Each unsure step I take
Trembling, stumbling as my spirit awakes
Lord hold my hand
Draw me nearer precious Lord
Then I know I will survive
Feeling your closeness guarantees security
My strength in crisis my hope when the tempest rise
Lord hold my hand
O for a faith that abides in me
Seen by others in moments measure
Living in my heart as priceless treasure
Growing as rippling tides flow in
Sustaining me from driving temptations whims
Precious Lord hold my hand
I cannot stand on my own
I'll never make it on my strength, for there is none
I find no comfort and nothing pleases
All I need, all I have, all I ever want
I find in Jesus
Precious Lord Hold My Hand

When We Pray Poem
Written By:
Doris Howard Surles
April 3, 1978
When we pray
How come we say
Lord, thy will be done
Then we go our way
Forgetting so quickly
What we've asked God's son
II
When we pray
Accept His way
Pray for love
Peace to everyone
For peace of mind
For all mankind
Let this be our prayer today

STORIES

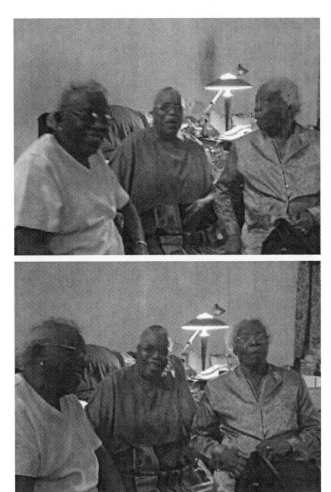

Writing all kinds of stories whether fact or fiction, short or tall is what I enjoyed most of all-stories about me and about you. Oh how my sisters love listening to my stories. Please enjoy my stories written just for you.

Christian Soldiers on Trial

Setting

I.

A. 8 persons-Male and Female. Representing each letter in the word Soldiers. Dressed in regular clothes. Underneath have the letters concealed and uniforms or have a robe over the letters and uniforms.

B. Have a group of accusers, shouting and hitting the soldiers.

C. (4) Four Guards must lead the soldiers to the Court Room and (4) four to try controlling the crowd.

Setting

II.

As the Soldiers and Guards enter the Court Room

There must be 12 Men and Women as jury (1) One Judge and bailiff (a court room set up)

Setting

III.

The Judge enters and the bailiff calls the court to order.

Scene I

A. The Christian soldiers walking along singing "I'm a Soldier in the Army of the Lord", "Onward Christian Soldiers".

B. The crowd is watching and clapping their hands to the songs and cheering the soldiers.

C. The accusers: seem to come from nowhere shouting and hitting

The soldiers shouting, "Arrest them". They are out of uniform. They sing and march as soldiers but they are out of uniform."

D. Some of the crowd

Yell: "Leave them be. What have they done?"

Accusers:

"They lie. They are not Christians Soldiers. Where are their signs or badges? Arrest them."

Guards Approaching the Christian Soldiers

"The accusers are right you know. You must have proof or you are considered to be out of uniform."

Crowd to the Guards and accusers

"Go pick on someone else."

E.

1st One of the Christian Soldiers: quoting from scripture: "Why we don't have to wear uniforms." (after Jesus died)

2nd Another Christian Soldier—"Speak on letting your light shine before men"

3rd Another Christian Soldier-From the Bible "Let your light shine. Ye are
    the light of the world."
4th Christian Soldier-From the Bible—"By this shall all men know ye are
    my disciples in that you love one another."
5th Christian Soldier-Speak about signs in Old Testament
6th Christian Soldier—Sign in the New Testament
7th Christian Soldier—Pharisees and wanted to be seen
8th Christian Soldier—Testify—"Need no sign to bring men, women, boy,
    girl to the saving knowledge of Jesus Christ."
Judge: "Order in the court."
Judge speaks—to Christian soldiers, "What proof do you have of these
    statements because there's a stiff sentence for calling yourselves soldiers
    without uniforms or identity."

All eight Christian soldiers hold up their Bible (King James Living Bible,
    N. I. V., different translations).
One Christian Soldier quotes and let the judge read for himself—"He was
    bruised for our infinity—"
Another read—"Put on the whole armor."
Sing: "God don't have no coward soldiers in His Band"
Song: "Am I a Soldier of the Cross" after everyone is heard.
Jury goes out—Talking among themselves
Brings a verdict of guilty
Accusers—Cheer when they hear the verdict
Judge—"Order the court to silence!"
All the Christian Soldiers stand before the Judge. The Judge's sentence is passed.
"You have heard the jury and I do hereby find you guilty and I sentence you
    to life!" (the accusers cheer)
Judge: "Silence!" He continues, "You, all of you, will spend life, eternal life
    with your Father in Heaven."
Christian Soldiers—"Praise God!" Singing "By & By When the Morning Comes"
Judge to the accusers: "Where do you think you are going?"
The accusers began to scream, "Have mercy on us!" (2 or 3 times)
Christian soldiers speak, "Judge, Your Honor, if it pleases the court. Please let
us give the plan of salvation to the accusers and everyone who will believe.
After all our duty is to bring everyone who believes in the Lord Jesus Christ
to repentance. Then we all can rejoice in Heaven together."

A Straw Hat for Johnny
Johnny was a poor and shy boy
Others tease him a lot
He seemed to always be last
But he accepted whatever he got
While standing in line to receive his gift
All the others had pushed him back
When he got to the front
All the gifts were gone
Except a torn dirty straw hat
He took the hat and put it on
He thanked them with a smile
Everyone laughed and shouted
Look at that
How can he smile and say thank you
For the dirty torn straw hat
Well you see said Johnny
My Pop had a hat like this
At first it was brand new
Soon it became dirty and torn
From the summer heat
And the morning dew
The sweat from my Pop's brow
Made his straw hat lose its shape
I never forgot that old straw hat
Even until this day
I'd always ask to wear my Pop's hat
Sometimes I'd try it on
I tried to make it fit
Pop would say just be patient son
Wait 'til you grow up a bit
Well my Pop died and we moved away my mother seven sisters and brothers
And I never saw that old hat again
At night I'd lay in bed
Wondering if that old torn hat
Would now fit my head
So you see it's not the old straw hat
I see today but the one I saw years ago
It may not be my Pop's old hat

This I'll never know
I said thank you because I'm rather proud of it
At least I have something to remember
And now the old hat fits

Determined to Get It On
I used to wear this outfit
When I was kind of large
Well let's say fat
So I pulled it out this morning
And said, now I know I can wear that
So I began to pull it on and I was not aware
I had to pull and tug and wiggle so hard
I had to stop and sit in a chair
After awhile, I got my breath and said
I am not giving up on this
Pull, tug, pull, tug
Wow I thought I was doing the twist
Then I said, what is wrong with me
I am not using my head
All I have to do is take a deep breath
And lie down on my bed
Everything will be fine
Now that everything is flat
Tugging, smiling, holding my breath
Again I said I know I can fix that
Well to my surprise I soon realized
This is not easy. It's hard
It's like putting a whole large delicious fruit
Into a little tiny jar
Well I'm determined no matter what
Again and again I'll try it
I forgot how long
I even forgot when or where I bought it
I wonder why I did it
Was I on a diet or just fooling myself along
I sure can't remember when I wore a size seven
Or even a perfect ten
Yet I'm determined to get it on
So I tried again and again
Finally I got it on
I'm glad this outfit stretches
I don't know where everything went
I didn't suddenly get thin

But now I know how a weenie feels
When all packed in a tiny skin
I wonder if my getting out
Will be as hard as getting in it
OK, I'm still determined
I have made up my mind to eat right
Not get up tight about certain things I can't wear
I'll just fix up all the extras
And my eating I must take care
Until that time, I'll go and find
An outfit that's my size
Keep the outfit that I squeezed into
As a reminder or one day be surprised
Also stay determined
Even with a grin
To look into that wardrobe
Try that little outfit again

Farewell Sophia

It was the beginning of September and everyone was preparing for the
months ahead. Back to school and ending summer vacations. With mixed
emotions, many new decisions had to be made. Sophia and Ty were
among the rushing crowd at the bus depot. Sophia reluctantly headed back
home to Boston and Ty remained home in the windy city of Chicago. It's
2:45pm and the wind is calm and a very pleasant 79 degrees.

Sophia is hurrying to get to the bus depot. She has written Ty a long letter
explaining her reasons for going alone.

Dear Ty,

Please don't be angry or sad. You know I would never try to hurt you.
Please read my letter written to you with your heart and mind, then try to
understand. You know how much we love one another and we have kept
our love strong for one year. I hope it will continue to grow even stronger
in the years to come. This letter is very difficult for me to write Ty, and I
am so sorry, but I was afraid to tell you in person because I didn't think
I would be strong enough to face you without giving in to your wishes. I
thought about this for a long time. I even had a long talk with my parents
concerning my decision. But, I see you made it to the bus depot before I
got on. I am sorry darling, please don't be hurt. I feel sad too, but I know
this is best for both of us. "But Sophia," said Ty "how can you do this?
You can't. You just can't do this. You will be in another state at another
school. We have always been together. I cannot bear being away from you.
I look forward to our walks from school and studying together, holding
hands and making plans for our future together. We were going to get
married and have our own family. What happened? Who changed your
mind?"

"Ty," said Sophia, "Remember when we ran away together? I realized then
we were in love, but not acting like young adults. We were being very
childish and selfish . . . thinking only of ourselves and our own feelings.
We can't build a lasting relationship this way. There are many others to
consider. Our families, friends, our parents who worked hard putting us
through school." "But Sophia, I can't. I know I can't make it without you
here with me."

"Yes we can Ty" said Sophia, "I know we can make it. It will only be for
three more years. Time will go swiftly if we put our minds to it. We will
see each other during holidays and summer vacations. We will write each
other, send pictures, and call on the phone. Ty, if we study hard and think
positive about our plans, we can do what we started to do, except we will

be on hold for a little while. I need you to understand Ty, and be strong with me and for me please."

"But Sophia, darling Sophia, why can't we be here together. Get married now then go back to school. Then we will not have to be apart."

"Ty" said Sophia, "miles will not stop us from loving each other and if we want to have a family, and we will, then we should plan for a family first such as education, jobs, and some money. Babies are sweet and costly."

"Sophia" said Ty, "I am standing here looking at this letter and listening to you. I cannot believe it. It's as though I'm dreaming, but I will do as you requested. Promise me you won't forget about me. Promise you will never stop loving me, and I will always love you. I miss you already, my darling Sophia." "I feel the same Ty. We will make it together. I know we will because this is the right way."

"Sophia, remember your pet name I gave you?" "Yes Ty, you always call me 'Muffin'. And what do I call you Ty?" asked Sophia. Ty answered "Roc". We gave each other pet names because this is our way of having special things no one else can take from us. Roc means tough and strong. Muffin, soft and sweet. These are the special things we see in each other and that is what we will think about everyday and night. Before we know it, we will be together forever.

Father and Son

"Get whatever you want. It's on me," said DJ's father, David, who wanted to butter DJ up.

"Oh, for real. I hope you know what you're doing, Dad," said DJ After the order was placed, DJ and his Dad sat and prepared to have lunch. "So, DJ, tell me how are things going in the apartment?" "Oh, Dad, our apartment is the bomb. It's a little crowded, but it's working out. We're getting our work done, but our party is on, too." All DJ's Dad could focus on was "a little crowded".

How can I tell DJ my problem now, he thought. A lot of thoughts were rolling through David's head while DJ was rattling on. "So, Dad, when are you to come peep at the apartment?"

"Dad!" "Huh?" David thought to himself, sooner than you think. "How are you and Mom coming along?" David didn't answer. "Is everything all right, Dad?" "No, son, everything is not all right. In fact, everything is downright terrible." "What are you talking about?", asked DJ "Son, your mother and I have been having problem after problem and your mother thinks it best if we just stop right where we are and go our separate ways." "Do you mean you guys are going to separate?" "Worse, son, your Mom and I are getting a divorce." "A divorce. Dag", was all DJ could say. "What are you going to do, Dad?"

"I don't know. She put me out, son!" "Dag, Dad, that's busted." "I don't have any place to go and the way my credit is looking, I can't find a decent apartment immediately and I need somewhere to stay now." "What about your friend, Stan? He has an extra room." "Stan's daughter just moved in with him." "Well, what about Jim, Larry, Tom . . ." and the list kept going on.

"No, no, no, son." "Well, I don't know what to tell you, Dad. I sure wish I could help you."

"I'm glad you said that. How about I stay with you and your friends for a bit until I can find an apartment?"

"Dad, I don't think you would like it there." "Well, you were just talking about how nice it was."

"Oh, I was just saying that so you wouldn't feel bad for me." DJ was feeling really bad for dissing his dad, but he couldn't let his father move in to the apartment with him and his friends.

"Well, Dad, I have a 2:00 pm class and I can't be late. I'll call you tonight and we'll see if we can come up with any ideas." "Okay, son. I love you."

"I love you, too, Dad." DJ gave his dad a hug and left Burger King. When he walked out, he turned around and saw his father staring blankly in to space.

DJ went to his class, but all he could concentrate on was his Dad. He thought, if I didn't have anywhere to go, Dad would be the first person to take me in. Later on that night, DJ called his Dad's hotel room and told his Dad what he had been thinking and how sorry he was to try and play him. DJ asked his father if he would come and stay with him and his boys and David agreed. DJ had no idea that his father was as cool as he was and DJ's friends loved David.

David began to spend a lot of time with DJ and his friends and became a positive role model.

David's whole attitude took a change for the better. This positive change in David's attitude also helped rebuild a relationship with his wife. DJ had a family again.

What's With Elmer

He was very tall and thin, with thick busy hair. His teeth were uneven, very brown, with one tooth missing in the front of his mouth. His big brown eyes very lonely and sunken. He wore a pair of faded ragged blue jeans that was too short for his long legs and a long plaid shirt with only two buttons hung loosely around his frail body, its sleeves covering his hands. His unlaced tennis were dirty and ragged. He appeared to be shy and sad, but had a warm smile. His face was covered with pimples.

Alone he sat on the Church and neighborhood steps, playing jacks. Three weeks later a smaller boy ran up to him and said "Hi. I'm Stanley. Can I play jacks with you? What's your name?" After a long pause, in a high pitched voice, "M-M-My-My n-n-name is E-E-E-Elmer. I-I-I'm t-t-t-twelve too." Elmer was quiet after that.

Stanley didn't seem to care that as he talked to Elmer he just nodded his head yes or no. With his head down, hands thrust in his torn pockets, Elmer stumbled out "I-I-I like like like like t-t-t-to p-p-p-play basket b-b-ball."

"Come on then let's play basketball" said Stanley. Elmer finally looked up and saw that Stanley didn't care about how he looked so he began to talk more. "I-I-I d-d-d-don't h-have a basketball." "Oh" said Stanley, "But you can ask your parents to get you one, then we can play ball in the Church court yard.

"I-I-I d-don't have no parents. M-M-Mama died and I-I-I don't know where m-m-my Daddy is." "Sorry," said Stanley, "But I can ask my parents if you can come over to my house. I'm new around here and I need a new friend. What you say, will you come? Huh will ya?" Elmer smiled and said okay. He was so excited to be in a large clean house.

Everything is great. Stanley said out of breath "Come on I'll show you my room." Running up the carpet stairs he said to Elmer, "I have bunk beds. You can spend the night."

Elmer's face and eyes lit up for the first time. "This room is out of sight, Stanley. Check out all these tapes and train videos. Wow, look at the computer and the large TV. You are really living," said Elmer. He noticed Stanley's basketball. He even had a basketball hoop. "Man oh man."

"We can come back up here later," said Stanley. "Let's go down and eat. Hey, mom" yelled Stanley, "can we have pizzas?" "Yes, we can" said mom.

While everyone was enjoying pizzas, Stanley's Mom said, "Elmer, I'm a sign language teacher and I can help you with your speech if you like." "Th-ththank you" said Elmer. Stanley's Father interrupted and asked "Where do you live Elmer?" Elmer's head dropped and very softly he stumbled "In a big box on Scott Street." For the first time Elmer burst out in tears and Stanley and his Mom and Dad all felt sad for Elmer. "We are going to help you. Don't you worry. I'm a dentist. I'm going to fix your teeth then we are going shopping.

Elmer stopped crying and then smiled again saying "Thank you." "Man. Oh boy. You look great. I can't believe my eyes Elmer." The new gray suit, light blue shirt, blue and gray tie, patent leather shoes even the belt had a large 'E' for the buckle. Elmer also had new jeans, tennis, shirt, socks, underwear, haircut. "Wow" Stanley yelled. "Mom, Dad how did you do it?"

"Well, we are parents remember." They all laughed.

"Wait Elmer. We even have a bigger surprise for you. Close your eyes and turn around." When Elmer turned and opened his eyes, there stood a tall man about 7 feet. He grabbed Elmer up in his arms, hugged him and said, "I'm your Daddy son. I am Elmer Senior. These nice people gave me a job, got me in a wonderful program and we have a new place to live. You don't have to live alone in a box ever again."

"We can visit Stanley and his parents, they can visit us, and we can walk in the Church and neighborhood together."

What's With Elmer 2

I watched Elmer for two or three weeks playing on the Church steps and on the front steps in the neighborhoods. Elmer is 12 years old, very tall for his age. He has what appears to be acne on his face. His teeth are very uneven with one top tooth missing in the front of his mouth. His hair was uncombed with bald spots. Elmer seems to always be by himself on his knees drawing circles on the pavement or playing jacks.

He wore jeans that were too short and one leg on his jeans was torn. His plaid shirt was very large and hung loose from his shoulder because of two or three missing buttons.

I saw Elmer one Sunday while everyone was going in and out of Church. Elmer just watched. I noticed he had on the same clothes that I had seen for the past two or three weeks. His tennis shoes were very dirty with broken shoelaces. When he tried to walk or run his tennis would come off his feet.

He wore no socks.

One Sunday while watching from the van I saw a little boy come up to Elmer and say "Hi." Elmer didn't answer. "Can I play jacks with you?" Elmer seemed afraid. "My name is Stanley. I'm eleven. What's your name?"

Elmer said "M-m-m-my n-n-name Elmer." I listen closely. Elmer stutters very badly. He dropped his head, shifting from left to right as if embarrassed.

After awhile Elmer realized the boy did not seem to care nor did he make fun of him.

This seemed to give Elmer more confidence. I was careful not to be noticed from the rear of the van. With the window open and the blinds half shut, I could hear and see Elmer and Stanley.

Stanley said "How old are you?" Elmer answered very slowly. "I-I-I-I'm 12." With his head still down and shifting more he told Stanley "You can play jacks with me."

I noticed Elmer's warm smile as he looked up for the first time. He began to talk more to Stanley. Elmer said in a very slow, high pitched voice, "I-I-I-I like b-b-b-basket b-b-b-ball, but I-I-I ain't g-g-g-got no ball a-a-a-and no-no-no place to play."

"Ask your Mom and Dad to get you a ball. You can play in the Church yard with me and some more boys." "Elmer hesitated, scratching his head. All of a sudden he blurted out, "My Mama died and I don't know where my Daddy is. I stay in a big box on Scott Street."

Stanley was amazed. He just stood there as tears rolled down Elmer's face. Elmer started to leave but stopped and tearfully said, "You are the first person ever ask me anything. All the others laugh when I try to talk. You want to be my friend?" asked Elmer. "Sure," said Stanley. "If I asked my Mom and Dad if it's OK, will you come home with me to eat and play some games?"

I was anxious to see how Elmer was doing with his new friend, so I waited for what seemed like forever. One day in the same spot right in front of the Church I was almost ready to go out, and I spotted Stanley, but I didn't see Elmer. At least I didn't recognize Elmer. The boy I saw with Stanley was so different with a suit, hair cut, new shoes. Wow. Elmer had on a navy blue suit double breast and a blue and gray striped tie. His belt was brown with an 'E' on the buckle. His socks matched his tie and his shoes were brown matching his belt. Elmer's hair was close cut with a small neat part on the right side. He had very small rim glasses very stylish and they made him look like a very intelligent boy. When Elmer turned around toward the van I thought he saw me but he was admiring himself in the side mirror of the van. He straightened his tie and smiled that same warm smile only this time his teeth were all even and none were missing. Elmer turned to Stanley and said without stuttering "Thanks Stanley, for being my friend. If you hadn't asked your Mom and Dad if I could come home with you, I don't know what I would have done when it got cold. Just look at me. Gosh. Your Dad being a dentist fixed my teeth. Your Mom being a sign language teacher showed me how to speak. I never knew that stuttering was about emotional insecurity. They fed me and bought me new clothes and found my Dad. They told me they were going to help him get a nice place for us and send him where he can get help with his drinking problem. Now Stanley instead of playing around the Church, I can go in the Church. I can also go back to school and play basketball. When I graduate, I'm going to college to become a chemist and a professional basketball player. Thanks my friend."

"I will never forget you and your parents. I hope we go to the same school and college."

I watched the two boys walk together in Church. What a great story. I'm glad I chose Elmer to observe.

Baby
My Child I Know How You Feel
She never thought she was a star
It's her children all over the world
Children near and far
She never ever seeks wealth and fame
She said it seems to come with a lot of pain
Instead of pride it brings shame
It reminds her of an ugly past
It brings back nightmares
That last and last
She lived from one condemned house to another
With drunks on the corners
And lying in the gutters
A sickly mother and elderly Grandmother
The only joy she finds in fame
Is the mention of Grandma and Mommy's names
The children she loves and sees along the way
Is the reason she is alive today
She said some days I wonder why I even bother
She ask what's the use
She is haunted by her father's sexual and verbal abuse
To this day she has no husband
Or even a boyfriend
When will I have peace Mommy
When will the nightmare end
She wishes she could tell of a wonderful life
A life of stories with sugar and spice
If I could remember just one day or night
She could remember that was nice
Not everything about her life brings pain and degradation
Except for her Mommy . . . her Granny
Her brother and the blessing of an education
She struggles each day to forget her past
Her pain, fears and shattered dreams
She always says . . . Mommy life is not what it seems
Every night this was my prayer
Lord while my Mommy's gone to work
And leaves me sound asleep

Please don't let me hear
The sound of my father's feet
But the Lord didn't hear me
Because as soon as Mommy was gone
My father would grab me from my bed and into his and my Mommy's room
Instead of having peaceful dreams . . . a sweet and restful night
I lay shivering, crying and scared to death
From what he did to me each night
No . . . oh no . . . I can never feel that I could be a star
Because what my father did to me has left an incurable scar
I have only one dream to come true
Then my life would be fulfilled
To have my program and my children
This to me is real
With the help of God and the support of others
This is why I work so hard
This is why I strive
To send the message loud and clear
What you are looking for is already inside
The terrible things my child experienced is true and very real
In court and even afterward
He acted as if it was no big deal
My child lay in a fetal position crying scared and still
Afraid because he threatened her
If you tell, your Mommy and Granny will be killed
She was convinced without a shadow of doubt
Afraid for what would happen
If her brother ever found out
She thought that God didn't hear her
She wondered what she had done wrong
But indeed God was listening
It was God who kept her strong
It took a lot of courage my child
To endure it all alone
Now I know why you held me so tight
When I would take you in my arms
When you finally broke down and told me
I promised you right then
This demon . . . good for nothing dog

Would never hurt you again
This happened to my dear child many years ago
But the nightmare still lingers
How long you'll never know
I'm so very proud of you
In spite of all your pain
You strive to achieve . . . determined to succeed
Keep the faith my child
To the end
She always wears a beautiful smile
In everything she does
Her saying is that the smile I wear
Is not for me
I'll always have a smile for you
Love you (Baby) Dedicated to my daughter Gaynell

CUTIE: A MOTHER'S DAY GIFT FOR YOU

It was a gift for Mother's Day-a cute sweet little Beanie Bear to touch a Mother's heart

When I was in the hospital I was pleasantly surprised. My daughter she purchased for me this beautiful little bright eyed stuffed animal, the cutest I've ever seen. She was excited just like me.

But you see this is the story: Mother is in the hospital. She is very sick you see. That's why I got baby to make her feel better, a special gift from me.

My daughter, Gaynell, was on her way to my bed to give me a get well kiss. **Then something happened that we could never foresee. He had a bad accident. Oh, no, this cannot be. He fell on the floor and got ran over by my wheelchair.** She was not aware she had dragged my little Cutie under her power chair. I said, "Oh, my gosh you've killed it!" My daughter was still not aware, so she looked down, backed up and ran over Cutie again. Now, we were all upset.

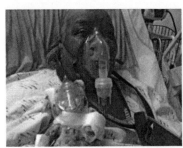 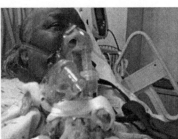 

I said, "We might call for a hearse". We smiled and said no instead we called my nurse. She came right away and said cutie did not look good at all. The nurse looked at the two of us and said, "But you know I'm crazy, too. I think this baby needs surgery, don't you? Don't you worry, watch what I can do. I'm a nurse we won't need the hearse!"

She ran from my room in a hurry, came back and said, "Don't worry like songs in a cup, after I'm finished with cutie, he'll be all fixed up." My daughter and nurse got everything needed from bandages to oxygen and they began to work on Cutie as if he was a human being. It was the funniest and strangest thing I've ever seen.

 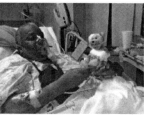 

Now he has to go to intensive care. He is really bad off as bad as can be. He was rushed off to have some major surgery. He looks so sad we really feel bad. Now he has bandages on his arm, shoulder, ribs and head. Things looked so bad I thought he was dead but he is a tuff little guy with a strong will to live you see.

Here are some pictures of Cutie. I think from what he went through, he really looks great! We would have taken him back and bought another, instead they fixed him up. Thanks to my daughter, my nurse and many others. Love you Cutie no matter what or where. Name it what you like, it so happens my Cutie is a teddy bear.

Now as you can see he's as happy as can be. Now that he's with his new Mommy his life is so sweet. Now baby has the very best seat right on his Mommy's heart. These two loves will never part Happy Mother's Day Mommy from your little baby's heart

A true story of tragedy by Momma Doris and Gaynell

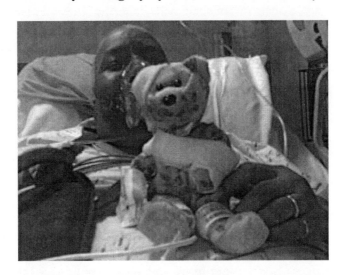

 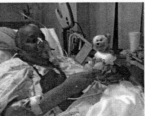 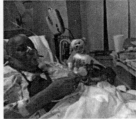

Dot's Corner

It has been my dream for as long as I can remember to travel, sing God's praise, and share good news which is the gospel. I would say to myself as a child I'm going to be a Missionary. Being the youngest of sixteen siblings with a father that had died when I was an infant prevented me from traveling. Mama was unable to provide this for ne so I began to travel in my mind, by reading and reading which lead me to writing. I saw the world in my mind. I would sit in the corner of our small house and dream. I realize it doesn't take much space to bring a smile to a face. Just write what you feel, it will not be erased. Dot's Corner is all I need to share my thoughts with you.

Fear

Fear won't leave me alone
It has haunted me all my life
It wakes me from my sleep
Whether I'm away or home
I was assured by someone I trust and know
You don't have to be afraid anymore
But I shiver when there's a knock on the door
Fear just won't leave me alone
This may seem like the very end
Let me tell you how this fear began
This is for the young and old
Fear will grip your very soul
No matter what anyone says
Fear is evil cold and hard
It did not come from the almighty God
Don't let it grab you it won't let go
It just won't leave you alone
I'll give you a true example
Until this day it brings me to tears
How someone I love dearly
Was damaged by this thing name fear
The one I promised a long time ago
Do not worry you will not be hurt anymore
My dear one answered I believe you
I know to me you wouldn't lie
But every time my heart beat
I can hear the sound of his feet
Not just the sound not heard by you
But remembering what he was coming to do
Not to read a bedtime story or tuck me in bed
But while doing unbelievable things
Threatening me if I told
Say a word your family is dead
Your Grandmother, Mother, your brother too
And that's not all I'll kill you too
This is the total devastation I had to get through
Now I have gotten better
The fear I had of that nightmare

Did not last forever
God has given me strength every hour
Now that one foul demon has no more power.
To Gaynell my Baby dear heart you are safe now

Happy Days, Unhappy Times
A True Story
Well, in a small 2nd floor east side apartment not realizing I was
considered poor. I look back now and think or say rather, no, I wasn't
poor. I may not have had some of the extras I have now, but I had the
necessities like food, clothes and shelter. I knew so much about God, what
He expected of me, but not knowing Him well enough to ask Him to take
me through some of life's experiences.
I woke up every morning looking forward to school. I guess I just loved
learning because I was not popular. I was never singled out or asked out
or any of those good things. I even tried to sing my way to popularity,
never happened.
Once in a while, especially in church, where I spent all of my leisure, I
got called to sing a solo. Before I could feel special, I was knocked down
because I did it too good or you think you are something. These remarks
were coming from the very ones I wanted to be around. Well, that was just
one of the many downs in my childhood life.
Being the youngest sibling of a very large family, sixteen altogether, I
was not the spoiled, showered with love, got my way type of kid. It was
Mama and church. That's it. I didn't feel sheltered and protected and
loved. I think as I look back I was loved, but everyone was struggling with
issues of his or her own; working, picking and choosing friends, trying
to find themselves. In the midst of all this, I had no remembrance of my
father, who was deceased since I was an infant. I found myself looking
to an older brother as my dad. I can't remember ever telling him this. I
just assumed this because he treated me like he treated his own children.
This made me feel safe. If I felt mistreated or troubled, I could and did
go to him. That didn't last very long because at the tender age of 10, my
father figure was gunned down on an early Christmas morning. Needless
to say, I was totally devastated. My mom and my love were so torn by this
terrible tragedy I don't think I ever knew nor thought what this actually
did to me. I felt so alone, frightened and no one seemed to notice.
Mama was a nurse and midwife. Let me go back again to my childhood;
about age 3 years. Yes, I can remember age 3. I remember the green and
white house with the porch swing; the large green lawn on the left side,
which housed the church. White church and in the back a large corn
field on the right side of my house, Mama's garden. I can still see what
my Mama called a ditch. Today we would call it a large trench or canal.
Anyway, we had a large wooden plank to walk across dirt streets. I still

see the bricks Mama collected to put in the front to make a walkway. I see
the proud and saintly woman; my Mama, white uniform, blue cape with
a red lining blowing in the breeze. But get this. No one but God, herself
and me knew those black shining shoes had holes in the bottom. The inner
soles were made of layers of cardboard. Hot or cold that's how she had to
go to work. Sometimes, most of the time, midwife and nurse, my Mama
got no money. Most of her patients had no money. They gave material,
potato, corn, or just plain thank you. I pray one day I'll be able to pay you.
Thank God we lived in a day when you could grow your food in your
own garden. Mama had collard greens and turnip greens with large turnip
bottoms, corn, big red ripe tomatoes, string beans, cucumbers, and beets.
Now use the same imagination I use to see how family was. Food was
shared.
What Mama had was exchanged for something someone didn't have.
Families churned butter, canned peaches, pears, watermelon rinds, and
vegetables so year round there was food. All they had to do was make
yeast bread and fix some kind of meat. Meat that is considered unhealthy
today was plentiful then. All the hog and pig was used for food except the
hair.
Hog head, hog maws, hog chitlins, pig feet, pig ears, slab bacon, fat back,
pig tail, and of course, what was called stomach meat was used to season
the greens. Oh, boy, those were the days. My life consisted of going for
a while to Catholic school because I was what they called a charity case.
When you were unable to afford money for public school, you received
not the dressed up name we use today. It was charity. Everyone knew
who you were because the pink, green, and blue print material with the
small flowers and the Brogans shoes were all the same color and style.
I was blessed to have a Mama that sewed. My colors may have been the
same, but they were made different and starched to a T. Church has been
a part of my life all my life. I was never asked did I want to go. It was
automatically a part of me. Like breathing or going to sleep and waking
up. I remember how I looked forward to putting on what we called our
Sunday clothes; the blue bonnet, white shoes, and one of my Sunday
dresses; red or blue. All shiny, leg and body greased with the same grease
your mama cooked with, lard. It was used on hair, body, and food. Never
did me any harm. As far as I remember, everybody smelled the same.
One Sunday I was so excited I could hardly sit still. I was going to sing.
Sing a solo all by myself. I remember being too short to be seen so they
stood me on the big old wooden table. It was covered with a snow-white

sheet. Just to stand on that table was a lifetime experience because communion and offerings were what that table was used for. Oh my, and the song: "I Come to the Garden Alone". You know I could actually see that garden where someone named Jesus was there, walking and talking with me.

Sitting on my front porch in my swing was another highlight. Looking around at my Mama's flowers, watching neighbors sweeping, hanging clothes on the lines, washing boards making their own music as the neighbors washed, sang, and talked to one another. They were preparing for Sunday; the aroma of foods, planning the Easter egg hunt, beating the dust out of the rugs; all this going on at one time. Friday's another time I could hardly wait for dusk. That's about 7:30 PM. I could leave the porch and walk about 30 or 40 feet, which seemed like a whole big block for a little girl. At the corner was a large cart with a fire and smoke pouring from somewhere. I was too little to see inside, but it didn't matter because what I was looking for was far more exciting than the fire and smoke. You see this was the evening I had my quarter for my fish sandwich. Nothing excited me more. The fish was huge fish and two slices of bread and, of course, mustard. To my little hand it was almost too big for me to carry or eat, but I always managed. I never dropped one, but off to my swing I went to eat and sing. This was just about all of my life as a little girl at home. Of course, there was a tire swing made for me by my brother Daddy that was what I wanted to call him. He took a big tire, a car tire, and a big chain and made me a swing out in the backyard on a big walnut tree. I used to get in that tire and go around and around looking up in the sky and soar. Oh, there was one other what I called a divine experience. I say God because no one else could do it but Him. Another big house before my green and white house and on the right side of that house there was white sand. Pretty white sand. I would just go there to play in the sand. One day I found money, all change no paper money. Of course, this meant very little to me. I would go in the house and show Mama or my sisters, whoever was home. This was so unusual to them. They would go and dig in the same spot and other spots. Nothing. They got nothing. As soon as I would dig, sure enough, money; nickels, dimes, quarters. Of course, I never got rich, but I was popular as long as I dug up money. This happened until we had to move.

I wonder if anyone found my money spot.

We left that home in the country for another home in the city. Right away as soon as Mama and I got out of the cab, I began to cry. I said, "Mama,

I'm afraid. I don't like it here. I don't like the big city." There was no
green grass, no green and white house, no porch, no swing, and no tree
with walnuts. It was what I know now as trash day. There were large
baskets of ashes and trash everywhere. On the street, people were looking
out their windows. Some were resting their arms on pillows, yelling to
each other back and forth across the street. Kids were running up and
down, some were jumping rope others playing ball. Some were on their
steps playing jack and ball. I saw a game I was not used to. I never saw it
before. I found out later it was called hopscotch. I like that. I said I wanted
to learn that game. I found out right away the kids were not friendly. They
didn't welcome me to the neighborhood or their games. This made me
sad. They soon realized that Mama and I came from somewhere other
than another neighborhood. They checked out my clothes and they began
to laugh. They didn't wear a blue bonnet on their head. They didn't have
shoes on. They played in their bare feet. Some hair was neatly combed,
others weren't. When I spoke I was sorry I opened my mouth because
they also laughed at that. They began to let others know there was a
new kid on the block. The place Mama and I had to stay was awful. She
scrubbed and cleaned and washed and cried. We soon found a place of our
own. Not to our liking, but better than where we were.
We entered our small place from a side entrance, a large wooden gate, up
a flight of wooden steps, a small hallway. We opened the door and there
before us was two more steps, the front room, two windows, another
room, two windows, a large stove for cooking and heating. In that same
room stood a single sink right behind that sink to the left side was a door.
I opened it and there was one single toilet; just a toilet. "Mama," I asked,
"where are we going to sleep? Where are we going to take a bath?" We
had one more flight of stairs. At the top were two small rooms. They were
so low. That's when I learned that in this place they have what they called
attics. It was all right if you weren't tall. Thank God for a clean mother
and a mother with vision.
She and the rest of the family got busy; wallpaper, scrub brushes, lye
soap, bleach, and a large tin tub to bathe in. We were on our way to
dealing with our new way of living. Many nights no sleep would come. It
seemed I was afraid of everything and everyone. My first day of school
was horrible and many days to follow. With Mama working, sisters and
brothers working, I had to go on my own. Male relatives were the worst.
If they weren't fighting me themselves, they would push others to fight. I
didn't think I would live. I was so frightened. Telling didn't do any good.

At least it seemed to help when Mama would tell me," Pay no attention to the name calling. If someone hits you, you can't run all your life. You have to defend yourself." I prayed all night and day. It hindered me from doing well in school. They didn't give up. It was constant.

Then one day, the teacher discovered I could sing and act in plays. I thought at last I'll have peace. Wrong. I was pressured because I could do something well. Can you believe it infiltrated into the church? I never knew grownups could be so cruel nor did I know grownups would lie. I was so confused until there were times I thought I had done something, I knew I hadn't done. The way I closed myself away from the pain was music. My older siblings had every kind of record and when they were home and Mama was working, they would play those records; Tommy Dorsey, The Ink Spots, The Honeydrippers. Mama bought Rose Etta Thrope, The Golden Gate Quartet, and so many more. I learned the words very fast. There was one spiritual titled "I Hear the South Land Singing Little Children Come to God." As I struggled with trying to be accepted, I discovered I was going in to puberty (blooming) teenager. I would soon be going to junior high school. Now I should have been excited. Oh, no because I was told the higher grades and older kids were waiting for me. I was sick to my stomach with fear. Did I get better? Did I recover? Did I have the nerve to share my fears? No, no, no. Certainly not. I lived with it. Many times I lied pretending all was well.

I was popular, I had boyfriends and girlfriends; not so. I had one girlfriend that I believed was really a friend until certain others befriended her. Then I was done again. As the years passed, I didn't know how I got through those years. Those were the hazy, lazy years of fear and unacceptance. Now I said those days are behind me. Let me look forward to wonderful days of adulthood. I wanted a husband, eight children. You know, four boys, four girls, a nice comfortable place to live, a job like social work. You know, dealing with people. I always wanted to show people how they should be treated. The way I was treated made me want this kind of work more than ever. Now working and trying to cope with an older boss who couldn't keep his hands to himself. Going to business college was like going through the motion. My mind seemed to be everywhere except where I was and what I was doing. This one evening, I had just shared with the wife of my boss where and what he could do with his job and I explained to both of them why.

So I left my job. Being occupied with these thoughts, I stepped out to the street not noticing the light had changed to green. I heard this loud blasting horn. Looking up I noticed this huge truck which I later found to be an eighteen wheeler. When I looked up I noticed this very attractive man smiling. I think at that very moment, "He has picked his target". Anyway, he said, "If I had hit a pretty little lady like you, I think I would have to lie under a truck myself". I said, "Thank you, thank you". He said, "For what"? I answered, "Well, you didn't hit me and you blew your horn". How funny that sounds to me now. Well, from that he must have figured out I was not one that had any experience meeting a man. He asked if I would like a ride. "No", I said, "I'm almost home". Then he said something really strange. "May I follow you home? I want to meet your mother." Now he really has my attention.

"My mother? You want to meet my mother?" "Yes," he said. I looked at him for a long time and saw he was serious. I asked him, "Why? Why do you want to meet my mother?" His answer was, "I want to ask her if I can date you because I want to spend the rest of my life with you. I knew as soon as I laid eyes on you. You know I even have a nickname for you." I said, smiling now, "What is it?" He answered, "Pumpkin." I laughed. "Now tell me your real name." "What's yours first?" He gave me his name. I in turn told him mine as I walked up the street toward home. Sure enough he followed me. I told Mama what had happened. I told her he wanted to meet her.

I was old enough to date, but as I look back Mama didn't show the excitement I'd hoped. I had never known a man nor had I ever even thought about dating. He did not rush me in to intimacy, but was faithful. In visiting Mama and me, he pampered me with kind words and gifts for a while and when he finally asked me the question, I freaked. I said, "Mama always taught me and God says as well I'm supposed to be married first. That way if a child is conceived, I'll be doing the right thing." His answer shocked me. "That's what I meant. Let's get married." I was so happy to have someone I could call my own, to love me, to hold me, to listen to all the things I had experienced. Someone I could love, do all the things he desired, give him my all totally. Oh, I was in love as far as I knew love and I was willing to be taught all I didn't know by my husband to be. I had beautiful rings that I proudly showed off to everyone I saw. He took me along with his best friend to a small remote place where we were married. I thought this was the most beautiful and romantic time in my whole life. He explained he had to leave.

He had a very long trip and did not have time to plan a big wedding. My pastor at that time was away at a youth conference and we know we were to renew our vows when he returned. I was so happy nothing mattered. I would marry him in his truck if he had asked.

When we came back, we didn't go to a big hotel for a week, a night, a weekend. This was to come later. We were at a very nice home of his relative. He was so kind and patient, gentle and understanding. I on the other hand was scared to death. He convinced me that there was nothing to be afraid of. He would take care of me and he did. I trusted him completely.

Well, my first encounter we conceived a child. I was overjoyed . . . a husband and a child on the way. Oh, thank God. He is finally giving me some joy and peace. I don't know of anything else I could ask for. The only thing I wished for was that the long distance trips would become fewer because I missed him so much when he was away. Oh, God, don't let this happen. I am well into my pregnancy now. Everything seems beautiful, but it isn't. Oh, God, please don't let me hear anything that's not good. Please, God. This was a blistering hot day; a hot, hot summer holiday. I was so happy I didn't notice the heat much, but was thirsty. A family member called me to her place for some cold Kool-Aid. It was so good and refreshing. She was very quiet for she was most of the time very talkative. Finally, she turned very abrupt and said, "He knew he had ten dollars. He lied. He had it." I didn't know who or what she was talking about. I was afraid to ask because she seemed so strange. She said, "I'll fix him. I am going to tell. I am going to tell everything." She looked at me for a long time. I felt very uncomfortable. She took my hand and said, "Come stand by the window with me. I want to show you something." I could not figure out anything she wanted me to see, but I stood there. After a few seconds, I saw two people as they got closer. I knew one to be my husband. I started to call from the window. She urged me not to say anything, just watch. The relative said, "You know who that is." I looked at her and said, "Yes, that's my husband." "Yeah," she said, "but look." As I looked back out the window, I saw him put his arm around the woman whom I didn't know and he kissed her. I still didn't know what was going on. My husband was supposed to be on a long distance trip. Maybe it was cancelled or he got back early. Finally, the relative said, "While you are so happy about your marriage and your husband, you need to know. That woman he is with is carrying his baby just like you. She has an engagement ring on her finger to marry your husband. She already has four children." I felt faint. I was no longer hot from the heat or thirsty or anything. I was just numb. She said, "Wait. I'm not finished.

Your husband has a wife in a mental institution and his nephew is not his
nephew. He's your husband's son. Now, let's see how he likes finding out
you know." When I made my way down the steps to the street, she was
still talking but I didn't make out anything she was saying. I couldn't cry.
I couldn't think. I was like a zombie. I made it to his parents' house where
I sat in the dark and waited where I knew he would come. His truck was
still in the front of the house. When the door finally opened, he came in
humming some tune. He seemed happy. I waited until he got to the foot of
the stairs. He had a gun in his room. I could have used it on him or me or
both of us. Instead, I called him. It seemed as if I whispered his name, but
I startled him. He swung around. "Pumpkin, sweetie. What are you doing
here? I mean it's too hot. I thought you were home with your mother."
I didn't know what I was going to say. I didn't have a prepared speech. I
just opened my mouth and what came out surprised me. I simply asked,
"Why? Why did you lie? Why me? Why did you use me?" I repeated what
I was told and who told me. He stared at me in tears. I don't know whether
his tears were real or fake. He got on his knees and said, "If I had told
you, you would not have married me. You wouldn't have gone with me.
Please don't leave me." Still in shock I answered, "I trusted you. Where
there is no trust, there is no love." I walked out and felt my baby move
in my stomach as if it knew I was hurting. I think what helped me more
than anything was when I boarded the bus. It was crowded. People were
standing up. Yet almost to the rear of the bus was an empty seat. I didn't
understand. I sat down and after about a block or two, I attempted to look
out the window and the passenger sitting next to me was grossly deformed.
She had the features of a goat. Her face had whiskers like a goat, two little
horns protruded from her head and with a beard on her chin. Her hands
were hooves. I didn't see her feet. This dear woman; no one sat next to her.
I believe God allowed it. I said, "Hi." She said no one ever spoke to her or
looked at her without disgust. I said this is a pain you have for the rest of
your life. I have pain, too, but at least every day it will be less and less. Is
this all I have suffered to happen in my life? No. I have hardly scratched
the surface. When I said goodbye to the lady on the bus, I felt bad for her.
I thanked God for letting me feel her pain and not just my own. When I
started walking up the street, I saw my mother. She was standing in front
of the house waiting as if she knew something was wrong.
Mother held out her arms to embrace me. For the first time, I began to
cry. I told her everything. She cried with me. I had no one but Mama. My
pastor treated me like a bad disease. I was taken off the choir. I was not

allowed to sit or mingle with the other young people in the church. The
pastor and members said I was a bad influence on others. My baby was
called a bastard.

They didn't believe any of the pain I told them I suffered, but my mother
told me you will make it. Trust God and me, you, and your beautiful
baby will be just fine. I wanted to believe her, but the pain was so deep
I thought it would never stop. I have never to this day forgotten what
happened, but I got through it. I thought this would turn me against men;
never to trust one again.

You would think after that terrible experience I would not let another man
near me. Well, that didn't happen.

One evening, sometime later, my baby and I were on our way to the doctor
for checkups. I saw someone I had not seen in years. We played together as
kids. We went to school the same years. We competed in singing while in
school. This made me feel so good to see someone I knew. He was so glad
to see me, too. He took to my baby right away. This really made me happy.
We agreed to see each other. I had no one in my life at that time and he
said neither did he. I thought this was great. He said, "This is fate because
I always cared for you even when we were kids and often wondered where
and how you were." I couldn't say the same because I was head over heels
in love with someone that was no longer a part of my life. After seeing
each other for a while, we both decided to go steady (date). It went so
well and my child was so used to him and his family I really began to
love him. I must say it wasn't like my first love. Finally, he asked me to
marry him and I agreed. I felt confident this time I'll be fine because this
is someone I've known since I was a child. This is wonderful. Plus I had a
real wedding; a church wedding.

Things were good. We were like kids in my mind. I said this is happiness.
We went out with other couples. We danced, sang, went to movies, and
just stayed home having fun with the baby. I guess I could always call my
baby a baby, but after a few years another baby was on the way. What a
great feeling. Everyone was excited. I guess this was something I hadn't
noticed because my father-in-law was very strict. He was a person that
made sure things were done and done right. I loved him because he
was good to me and my children. He was not pleased with his son, my
husband, because he could not trust him to keep his word to tell the truth.
He found out he was not taking care of his family the way a man should.
I was in the dark about this until it was brought out in the open. It came
to the time when he, my husband, was told he had to go but me and my

children could stay as long as we wanted. Well, I left with my husband. I felt this was what I should do. I just knew he would do the right thing since we were living in our own place.

My mother-in-law was a wonderful Grandma to the children. I thought this would be the encouragement my husband needed to do the right things. What happened over the next few years is to this day beyond belief. I went to work so we could put our income together for a home and a car. I was home when he worked he was home when I worked. I felt this was perfect. We didn't have to pay for babysitting and our children were safe with both parents watching them. I never thought that my husband, my baby's father, would be the second nightmare in my life. I never dreamed or had any hint of what he was doing. This scum, I can't think of anything low enough to call him. While I was working, he was home sexually and mentally abusing my baby, his own child. How could he be so low? How could I have been so blind? I don't know how long or how often this went on, but when I found out I was devastated, sick I almost lost my mind. He terrified our child by saying, "I'll kill your mother, grandmother, and brother if you ever say a word." It's easy to frighten a child. I almost lost my mind. I had so many mixed emotions. I didn't deny him. I felt if I hadn't gone to work, I could have protected our child. Why? Oh, God, why? He was arrested. We tried to erase the pain, but it will haunt us all our life. We, me and my children, had a difficult time, but God took care of us. I had to stop working because I wanted to be with my children. I did hair in my neighborhood and I sold dinners throughout the community. I did so well we were able to move in to a home of our own. After years of suffering, we began to heal. Not all the way because that's the kind of pain you don't heal from. It was worse than my first nightmare because my innocent child was harmed. I finally went back to work. This is not the end of my life's pains, but I'll stop here. Life goes on. So does pain. I have so much more to tell. I know I'll write again.

This I'll share with, I hope, many of you. Next time I write, I'll probably call it Part Two. Who knows down the ages through the time of many pages as life takes twists and turns. What next I'll write, what else I'll learn? Who knows, it may be all happy times. Whatever the pages, they will be mine. Hopefully, someone can relate. Different times, different dates. They may have the same situations, may have similar situations. Maybe they, on pages, will share some of the times they felt despair. Someone will read it and care what's written on the pages there. Then they will decide one day or night to pick up a pen and begin to write—a true story.

Mama and a Light

I went to visit my Mama in the hospital
She was so very sick yet she was cheerful and bright
She told me a true story of an experience she had with a light
She said two women came in from the hallway
With hearts and minds of gloom
They said to Mama . . . it was a light
That caused us to enter your room
They asked Mama three or four times
Granny, are you alright
Mama answered . . . well, for a woman my age
I thank God for my mind and my sight
The women asked . . . how old are you
And what might your sickness be
The doctor says it's my heart . . . I guess he's right and
God blessed me to be one hundred three
And God takes care of me Mama said
The women were amazed
Here we are half your age and asking if you are alright
We just can't understand that strange and very bright light
We know it's not from the window because the sun
Is not yet out and there's no jewelry on you
No mirror or reflection of anything lying about
The women said . . . well, we'll go and let you get your rest
We can't understand how the light seems to come from where you're sitting
As if reflecting from your chest
It's so strange that light is coming from you . . . we saw it from the hall
Perhaps we will come in again
If you need anything, just call
We thought the light would hurt your eyes
It's so bright . . . that's why we came
Mama said . . . wait. Don't go. You may not get this chance again
Mama asked the women a question
Are you saved from sin
Well, said the women . . . we belong to a church . . . just lately we haven't been
We haven't been for many years
Mama told them . . . it takes more than that
To save you and stop you from living in fear
Mama told them how to admit they were sinners

And how to repent to Christ
How to accept Him into their hearts
And have a brand new life
The women soon left Mama's room
Encouraged and free from sin
They said Mama was such an inspiration
And they would never be lonely again
Well, I don't know how or why
These women saw a light
Nor where it could have gone
Only Jesus could have sent them
To my Mama's room
Only Jesus could have filled
Their hearts with joy
The hearts that were filled with gloom

Mama and Me

I love to hear my Mama tell of the many things she's done
How the spirit of God lived in her
How she raised us everyone
First she told me about my Daddy
How he got sick, so sick he died
How the many days and the long, long nights
She and her children cried
Mama told me even back then when times were really hard
She gained respect and had many friends
Because she served and trusted God
She told me when she became sanctified
Baptized by the Holy Ghost
Through visions and dreams oh this is the part I love most
Mama told me just before my brother was born
His birth came early and quick
She was thrown from a horse and wagon
As a result she became quite sick
Her doctor was out on another case
There was no way he could be reached
Her son was already born when the doctor got the word
When he arrived she was very weak
Mama said the spirit of God moved in her
To her He began to speak
God said child I'll show you the death of a saint
Instantly she was in a deep sleep
Then Mama began to tell me
The wonder that she saw when God's spirit put her to sleep
The sight she beheld was so beautiful
At first she could not speak
She could not describe what it was really like
Her whole body was limp and relaxed
She began to cry in a very loud voice
Oh Lord don't take me back
Mama said the almighty God took her spirit just like He said
God let her look on her natural body
As she lay in a coffin dead
The Lord showed her the beauty all around

A path narrow and bright
With beautiful flowers along each side
It was quiet not a sound or another soul in sight
Mama said it was as if she was floating
Her feet never touched the ground
She cried again Lord where is this place
Is it Heaven where I'm bound
The Lord showed all the places in this beautiful land
Churches, fields, hills, and mountains
Oh it was so peaceful and so grand
Again God spoke you cannot stay . . . you must go back
I have work for you to do
I did not know what the work would be
But I knew God would see me through
He brought me back to raise my children
Nine girls and seven boys
I was happy and never alone
I had a friend named God
Mama said that me and the Lord walked side by side
He told me everything to do
How to deliver children, pray for the sick
Clean their houses and bodies too
It was for Jesus not for money
Yet He supplied my every need
Some of the people I helped
Were very poor but were rich in many kind deeds
Mama said she served the people day and night
In her home and their homes too
No matter how busy she always took time
To thank the Lord for the work He gave her to do
Well I could never write all the wonderful things
My Mama said to me
Some were happy and some were sad
But when Mama told them I was very glad
Even now after ninety some years
She yet serves the Lord . . . she said the Lord made me free
I never regret the hard times . . . I'm as happy as I can be
So if you are ever lonely or discouraged

And happiness is impossible to see
Come and listen to Mama's true stories
Share them with Mama and me

On A Hill

On a hill not far away
Stands a bar, filled night and day
It's an eye sore of suffering and shame
There are those who love this old sinful place
It shows in every face . . . it don't matter that it's not safe
Drugs, drinks and lust
Brings them death and disgrace
Men and women swear, smoke, drink, and use all kinds of drugs
On the floor they exchange kisses and hugs
In the bathrooms they indulge in sex
Leaving children and families at home alone in a total wreck
How do I know all this goes on
When I don't hang out there
This comes from some I know and others who live near
It shows every day in every way
In their life and how they live
They just will not stay away from the sin
In that little hole up on the hill
When you go by there you can see they don't care
In their eyes is a hopeless stare
No future plans for that woman and man
But to wait for the day as soon as the good Lord
Wakes me up and lets me see another day
I'll be back in that bar on the hill not far away
The law won't close it down
Yet they are always around
Arresting someone everyday
Ambulance and sirens blasting
Fire and smoke from guns flashing
Knives and blood don't seem to matter
Some stand right there others duck, run and scatter
I wish I knew how they get through
When so many are hurt and dying
Homes are broken, harsh words are spoken
What a horrible life to endure
They don't seem to hear, they have no fear
They don't even seem to feel
All they have to look forward to is to get back to the bar on the hill

They say don't worry, I can take care of myself
Nothing's gonna happen to me
I'm here with my friends
That's not a sin I'll be home as soon as I can
Well I hope and pray that one day
I'll see the men and women realize with all the suffering and the pain
All those arrested, wounded, and killed
I hope they began to regret and will soon forget
And turn away from that awful place up on the hill

Panty Hose
Panty hose, panty hose
When were they invented
Panty hose, panty hose
Were they for me intended
They are small to queens
And they are for the ladies
Why don't they come in size kings
I know this may sound funny
Trying a pair on is a doosie honey
I wiggle and I jiggle
I wiggle and I squirm
I twist and I turn
I jump up and down
I do everything I can to get these things on
I lie on the bed and roll from side to side
Pulling and tugging
And they pop me on my thighs
After all the twisting, turning, pulling and tugging
And pain I had to endure
I don't have the energy to do this again
When I put my feet on the floor
To get ready to go out the door
There was a run where everyone could see
Queen size just ain't going on these thighs
I know some of you can't relate
I'm trying to get to church
These panty hose are going to make me late
I know this may sound funny
But it ain't no joke honey
Oh, goodness gracious
Lord have mercy
Panty hose, panty hose
You need to come in king size

Run Away

Jarvis heard the phone, but he did not answer it because he was angry. Talking to himself, Jarvis turned on the fan, kicked a scrap of paper on the floor and began to beat the toy train in his room. He threw his toys and clothes around as he was talking. "I am tired of my Mom and Dad always telling me what to do, She said, do your homework, Jarvis, take out the trash, Jarvis, clean your room, Jarvis, be sure to bolt the garage door, Jarvis, and do not forget to take your bath!" Have they forgotten that I am ten years old? "I am old enough to know what I want to do" he yelled. He changed the bulb in his lamp and made his Power Ranger and Joe-Joe clash. "Like I was saying," he said, "I do not have time to do anything I want to do. I want to play Nintendo, play with James' basketball and watch TV. I do have a life," said Jarvis. "Jarvis, don't forget to put your dirty clothes in the hamper" yelled his Mom. "I have to do something", said Jarvis. He sat on the side of his bed and thought, "I've got it! I've got it", yelled Jarvis. "I will scare the daylights out of them. I will run away. That's it! I'll just run away." Jarvis was laughing almost hysterically. He finally had found a way to get his parents off his back.

Jarvis began to get ready, thinking, "I can just see their faces when they call me for dinner and I don't answer. Then they will come running to my room and I will be gone. Ha! Ha! Ha! Ha! Jarvis laughed. I'm not going very far, so I don't have to pack. However, my parents don't know that. Very quickly he grabbed a comic book, tiptoed down the stairs, took some cookies and put his skates outside the back door. Suddenly, his Mom called from the dining room. "Is that you, Jarvis?" "Yes Mom," answered Jarvis. "I'm just taking the trash out." He opened the back door, locked it behind him and put the trash in the large can. He tucked his comic book and cookies in his pocket, picked up his skates and off he went.

Jarvis decided to go to the big park, which was just a few blocks away. "I'll put on my skates here," he said as he sat on the park bench. Jarvis was careful not to let Miss Ally and Mr. Jake see him. They were his neighbors, who walked their dogs (Spot and Jasper) everyday at the same time in the big park. Jarvis began to wonder why people called this the "big park". It sure doesn't look big to me, he thought. He looked up at the tall beautiful trees and ate some cookies. Suddenly, he heard voices in the distance and decided to skate away before he was seen. He skated for what seemed like hours before he realized how tired he was. He saw a place in the park where there was grass and a tree. He stopped and decided to rest on the grass for a while.

He watched the squirrels and the birds for a while, but he was so tired he
went sound asleep. Suddenly a loud squeaking noise startled Jarvis awake.
He jumped up and looked around, but he saw nothing. He realized he had
made three mistakes. He had slept until it was dark, he hadn't brought
a flashlight and he hadn't brought a watch. He realized something else,
though. It was dark. "It is very dark," said Jarvis. Now I know why this
is called "Big Park". I don't know where I am. It's different at night and
scary. The tall beautiful trees now look like long scary arms, reaching out
to grab me. I can't skate and find my way out of the park because I can't
see where I'm going.
It's cold. I forgot my sweater and I'm out of cookies. What am I going to
eat or drink?"
While pondering these thoughts aloud, Jarvis noticed that he didn't hear
or see any cars. He began to walk. He continued to walk for a long time,
a very long time. "I don't know how long I've been walking," said Jarvis.
He began to cry. "I don't feel so big now," he cried. "Oh, God! I wish
someone would find me. Maybe Miss Ally and Mr. Jake will walk their
dogs late or maybe someone will take a short cut through big park.
"Please! Please! Mom, Dad, find me!" he yelled. Strange sounds and
shadows were all around him and he felt like he was going to die. "Help!
Help! I'm lost!" he screamed. "Mom, Dad, find me!" He screamed until
his voice was gone. Sitting on the ground just about to give up, Jarvis heard
voices and thought, "I must be dreaming." The voices came closer and
louder. Finally, he heard his name. "Jarvis, Jarvis, are you out here?" Jarvis
could not believe it. The voices were his Mom and Dad's. He saw lights
flicking in the darkness closer and closer. Jarvis answered, "Over here!
Over here!" When we finally saw each other, Jarvis ran to his parents and
into their arms. I never realized how much I love and missed my parents.
They looked at me and said, "You have been punished enough Jarvis."
Mom and Dad took me home gave me hot soup and crackers a tall glass of
lemonade. I asked my parents to please forgive me. They didn't have to tell
me to take a bath, because I was ready to get into a tub of warm sudsy water.
It felt so good! After my bath I was ready for bed, but first I had to answer
a question. Why did I run away? I thought I knew more than my parents
and that I could take care of myself. What did I learn thought Jarvis. I
learned that it is not smart to run away, it's dangerous. In fact, thought
Jarvis, it's better and safer to be in the house, doing my chores than out in
big park lost and frightened. I thank God for my Mom and Dad. I know
they will not tell me anything wrong.

Sixteen Siblings, One Pair of Shoes

There I lived, the youngest of sixteen siblings, in the quiet, small house, on a tall, tall hill in the back woods of North Carolina. My mother, nine girls and seven boys. My father was deceased.

One day, Mama, as we called her, was trying to decide how she could do something really unusual; something she had never heard of or ever done before. She cooked, knitted, crocheted, ironed, played with us, and visited a sick neighbor. With all these things done, what could she possibly do? We were all wondering what Mama was up to. She only told us it would be good for all of us.

When she told us to get ready for bed, we all hesitated. "Mama," we asked, "Can we stay up to see what you are going to do? Please Mama?" "No," she said, smiling. "I can only say it will be good for all of you." We took baths and brushed our teeth very slowly, peeping and watching, but we saw nothing. Finally, we drifted off to sleep.

The next morning when we awoke, Mama called us to the large family room. "Sit down" she said. "I will show you what I have done. Cover your eyes and don't peek." So, we closed our eyes.

"No talking," said Mama. "No matter what you feel, not one sound now." "OK, Mama" we said.

After awhile, we felt something very soft and warm, but we promised not to talk. So, we just waited with our eyes closed. Finally Mama shouted, "Open your eyes now! All of you open your eyes!" And when we did, we looked at our feet. We had on beautiful, warm, soft shoes.

"Mama" we shouted! "Mama, they are wonderful. How did you do it? How Mama, did you do it for sixteen of us? Not one pair" we said, "but sixteen?" Mama smiled and said, "It would take a long time to tell you how. But, I'll tell when you take them off, what you see inside."

Mama had written in red thread "One Pair for Sixteen Siblings." "We do not understand, Mama." She answered, "Haven't you heard, One pair fits all?" We all had a good laugh and a good day.

What?

I was looking for Gabby and for Matt
under the bed I said where are they at?
They're under the bed getting the bat
Watch out Matt, don't step on the cat
And don't forget to put on your hat
My hat said Matt, what is dat
Oh don't be silly said Gabby to Matt
Hurry up said Matt cause the last one out
is a big fat rat, Oh, Yuck! I hate that!

THOUGHTS OF THE DAY

I write all the time. I write my thoughts as they come into my mind. I wanted to share with you some of the thoughts of the day as they came my way.

Age
Now that I am up in age
I find myself almost in a rage
Most of family is no longer around
Valuable information cannot be found
Family history not known
Prosperity is no longer owned
Portraits last some faded and torn
Leaves me wondering about my past
Where did we start from
Memories are great but they fade so fast
I see families' on TV
Makes me feel like that could be me
How my past could be

Amazing Life Changes

I live in what some call the hood it's amazing I thought I never would live in this neighborhood. When I was a girl my mom and me walked these same streets they were so beautiful clean unique marble white steps and wrought iron fences. Policemen walking the beat, this building was a mansion then and only the rich and the well respected was allowed to enter in.

Mama and me would say to each other one day we will live like this. Beautiful houses, cars, and those marble steps. It was something you could not miss, now what is so amazing is how life changes as years and years go by people move and people die and neighborhoods become run down. We don't always understand why. One wish I made as a child now is a reality. Mama died and with pride I can say I live in a mansion some call the hood, you see the mansion became a part of the hood. Someone had an idea to make it a senior citizens apartment. So I can say dreams do come true I live in a mansion in the hood.

A City of Twins
Look two identical girls
In two identical hats
Two identical boys
With two identical bats
Two identical women
Two identical men
Two identical houses
Two identical friends
Two identical teachers
Two identical schools
Two identical wise ones
Two identical fools
Two identical witnesses
In this great city of twins
Needs the only One Savior
To save them from their sins

A Dream
I dreamed that I was walking home
When suddenly I was flying
My feet and hands were waving and turning
I was laughing instead of crying
I don't remember how I got down
But would like to dream of flying again
Maybe to the moon or through the blue lagoon
Maybe visit some far away friends

A Rock and a Hard Place

Life is full of uncertainties
We don't know what we will face
Sometimes we feel like there is no place to turn
We are between a rock and a hard place.
I've always heard this quite often
Someone mistakes has brought disgrace
They don't know right from left
Between this rock and a hard place
Too many times we fail to see
The space that's in between
This is a secret place where God dwells
Although His face is unseen
We must dwell in this secret place
It's there where we'll find the most high of the Almighty's embrace
He will be our rock in that empty space
And protect us when we find ourselves
Between a rock and a hard place

A Special Room

Our house is a special place
A place we can call our own
We give God all the praise
Because He made our house
Our home
In our home we have six rooms
A basement, front and back yard,
But inside is a special room
I call this a special room
Without it a lot would be missing
This special room is in every house
This room is called a kitchen
Our kitchen is such a special place
This is my favorite room
This is my special place to go
And use my knife fork and spoon
I really do love this special place,
I call it my special spot.
I can show my friends and family
All the talents I've got.
Everyone may be busy
Or just watching something on T.V.
But when they hear the pots
And pans and smelling the food,
They all start watching me
Bless our home
Each day I pray
Bless my kitchen
In a special way
My kitchen is where
I show I care
In every meal
That we share
It's not only where I cook
Or try new recipes from a book
My kitchen is where I can be myself.
Putting things away and stocking the shelf.
It's not just a room

Where I go to eat
My kitchen is a room
Where my family always meet.
God gives us foods
Of every kind
He gave us this kitchen
With me in mind
That's why I thank God
For our home
And for giving me a kitchen all my own

A Thought from a Dream

I dreamed about my dear old mother
She was knocking on our door
She was with three other women
Whom I did not know
We were running in all directions
Trying to straighten up inside
We didn't expect our mother and company
We couldn't just up and hide
Then the dream seemed to change
We were no longer at our house
We were among a crowd of people
Who made strange noises with their mouths
I noticed my mother and company
Were dressed in beautiful black lace
And my mother had the strangest look
That I've seen on any face
Then suddenly she began to cry
Like her tears were for all the nation
She stopped crying
And started to sing an old, old hymn
HE'S THE JOY OF MY SALVATION
I suddenly woke up
I began to write
I thought about what I had dreamed
Suppose that was Jesus at our door
And found our souls unclean

Ain't Gonna Never Get Old

Ain't gonna never get old
I got my faith and I got my dream
Ain't gonna never get old
Gonna do it my way and keep it clean
Everybody this song's for you
Senior and retirees too
Whenever I can't sing and play
I'll keep on feeling the same way
My music and dreams will live on
Cause my music will keep me free
Ain't gonna never get old
Everyone's going to remember me
People will sing it after I'm gone
I ain't gonna never get old
Ain't gonna never get old
I'm gonna keep on singing
Ain't gonna never get old
I'm gonna keep on swinging
Ain't gonna never get old
Me and my music will live forever
Mentally I'm gonna keep it together
Ain't gonna never get old
Come on people
Let's get it together
'Cause I ain't gonna never get old

All about Christmas

Tell me the story about Christmas
Sing me the song of His birth
Write me a poem about Christ the Savior
And the peace He brought to Earth
Oh not now dear child
Do not bother me
Can't you see I am busy decorating the tree
I have so much to do
Wrapping presents, baking cakes and pies
Needing someplace for my presents to hide
My body is aching from head to toe
I can't stop now
I have three more places to go
I must hurry because the weatherman said snow
I know you want a story, a poem or a song
But I have been busy all day long
To worry me like this is selfish and wrong
You should be more understanding
Try to be strong
Lord, I have got to sit down
The aches and pains have not gone away
I guess I'd better get a sweater
I've been kind of chilly all day
I feel so dizzy I can hardly see
I wish I had someone to read to me
Something nice like a poem or a song
Something to help me carry on
There's my child, come here to me
I'm dizzy and burning up, thirsty as I can be
Come read to me or sing to me
Bring me something cool
I'm so sorry, I'll bring you a cool drink
Then I must hurry off to school
As I sit here sipping the cool mint tea
I thought to myself
What Christmas really means to me
It came upon a midnight clear
It was a silent night

Away in a manger
Poor little Jesus boy
Was born to be our light
Joy to the world
We all can sing
Glory to the new born king
Tonight I will lay my child to sleep
I'll sing a song of a child so sweet
I'll read the story of His birth
I'll say a poem of peace on earth
Then I heard the bells ring
The cheers and the shouts
Halleluiah, halleluiah
To the new born king
I said with a smile, that's what Christmas is all about

Be a Good American

Be a good American
Lend a helping hand
Show other nations how glad you are
To be in this great land
Be a proud American
Help keep our country clean
With humble pride always strive
To keep America the land of our dreams

Black History Month

This is the time we reflect and honor our heroes
As we think about the heroes
That were long ago and the wonderful things they did
We must also reflect on the heroes we live among
We have new heroes that we can see and touch
Some of our heroes are physically doing fine
Then from the crash, the ash and rubble
Our heroes are dead or dying
We cannot name them all and
We can't tell one from the other
Because we watched them on that terrible day in horror
Everyone was the same color
Men, women, even children
Those alive and dead
This month and every single day are heroes
The ones on land, in the sea and skies
Harriet Tubman, Martin Luther King and everyone who served and died
We will never, never forget them
We acknowledge them with great pride
While we are celebrating, let us not forget the heroes we see each day
Our pastors, fathers, mothers, and grandparents.
Think of the role they play
Teachers, friends, and family
Who help us along the way
Are all our wonderful heroes
In a very special way
God has crowned our good with brotherhood
Let us be thankful for the heroes who passed on
Thank Him for those here now
Thank Him for the ones that are on the way
For we will always have our heroes
They will always be strong and survive

Bubbling Brown Sugar

I'm not a sugar beet
Crystallized and sweet
I'm not a material
That an apple wears for a coat
Or some sugar daddy
Who owns me, houses, cars, and boats
I'm not a sugar berry
An orchard or pine
In a sugar house
That's not even mine
I'm not an artificial, converted maple syrup
That has no flavor
If mixed with earth
I have uncoated sweetness
Since the day I was born
I am brown sugar
Beautiful, intelligent and strong
Strive to be right
But will admit it
If I'm wrong
I love the right kind of attention
But very careful how I choose
Determined to win
Yet strong enough to lose
So if you meet me some day or night
You better make sure you are Mister Right
This brown sugar
I'm none of these things
So what's the point
Do you have something you can flaunt
Well, I'm glad you asked
I don't mean to brag
But I'm brown sugar and this is a fact
I am sweet as sugar
And brown as a beet
I am crystal clear
Yet you can't see through me
I'm as subtle as an apple

This comes naturally
I am a brown sugar lady
I am not one you can own lady
Is very rare
She will not tolerate mistreatment
Only tender loving care
Dedicated to Lorraine McKenzie Blackshire

Cards

Let me make your cards a book
Any time you like
You can take a look
Cards like pictures
Are delightful to see
And they bring refreshing memories

Christmas

C is for the Christ child
   Born on Christmas day
H is for the holy child
   Who in a manger lay
R is for righteousness to the world He brought
   Rest, comfort, and peace as the wise men sought
I is for the inn
   Where there was no room
S is for the stable, dark and filled with gloom
T is for the treasures they brought
   When they heard of Jesus' birth
M is for the three wise men
   Who shouted with great joy
A is for the angels who came from the heavenly sky
S is for the Savior of the world
Glory to God on high
Merry Christmas/Happy birthday Jesus

Don't Take My Fun Away
Don't take my fun away
Be my sun
Oh please stay
Don't take my fun away
I won't let you take
My fun away
Rain don't take my fun away
Snow go away
I have something outside
To do today
Even so I have to say
I won't let you stop me today

Doris

Doris, who are you
Who am I
What can you possibly be
Well, for one thing I know for sure
I have determined that
Only
Righteousness
Insures
Salvation
For every Doris in the nation
What am I
I am saved
I am bountiful
And I am God's creation
I am short so some may think
I am tall in many ways
I am witty
And sometimes I give myself pity
I have learned to value the days
I sing, I dance, I think, I sleep
I am well,
I eat, I laugh, I weep.
I am quick,
Sometimes I am sick
God has given wisdom; He used no gimmick, prank, or trick
Doris, who are you really
You write what you do
But I want to know who you really are
I am a mother, a daughter
A fatherless and motherless child
From a child Mama fed me Jesus
She said, "God will be your advisor when I am unable to advise you.
He will guide you"
So whoever I am, whatever I do
Ask my father, He will tell you
He knows me better
Than I know myself
This is who I am
And what I am
And will be until my death

Dream

Dreams are made for me and you
But dreams don't always come true
Dreams we dream aren't always the same
Sometimes they don't have a name
But we keep on dreaming they still remain
We dream anytime and anywhere
Some dreams are pleasant some nightmares
Some we can't remember
Some dreams we wish to forget
Dreams just keep coming even with regret
How can we stop dreaming
Especially the ones that are unkind
The ones that never come true
Yet they haunt us all the time
They will come day or night
Whether we like them or not
Dreams are a part of our living
Sometimes dreams are all we got
So keep on dreaming

Evil

Evil try to describe it
Try to understand its meaning
Evil don't need an excuse
Evil knows no good
It thrives and grows on abuse-
Evil needs no reason
It has no special season
Its middle name is treason
Defining it is hard
Evil has no regard
It has a powerful enemy
And very well it should
The only thing that scatters it
Is an old remedy called good.

From a Child

I cannot put the words together
As most grownups can do
But I can say with all my heart
I really and truly love you
And though you are not here to be with me
This I promise you
I will be the child and proud adult
Just the way you want me to be

Girl, Girl, Girl
Look at you . . . you ain't the same
You say you're grown
You're stuck on yourself
Got you somebody . . . got no shame
Fooling yourself to death
Girl, Girl, Girl
Get a hold of your mind
Look in the mirror of your soul sometimes
Stop being so arrogant and full of pride
Who got you full of ice inside
What you going to do girl
When you are down and out
You ain't never had it bad
Girl you don't know
What it's all about
You think you and your man
Is all that matters
You think you got it going on
No matter who gets shattered
Girl you got your groove going on
Girl you riding high
Ain't nothing stopping you
You're reaching for the sky
You don't care girl
If I live or die
You have no more shame
Girl is grown
Got to prove she can do it on her own
Forget about all the support she was shown
Can't touch the girl . . . the girl is gone
Nothing you can tell her
Time's running out
I tried to compel her
She hears me but she ain't listening
Too bad . . . too sad, Girl, Girl, Girl
She's going . . . going . . . gone

God's Angels
Mommy lay me down to sleep
Sometimes Daddy do
They always tell me . . . don't be afraid
God's angels are watching over you
When I grow up I want to be
Like Mommy and Daddy too
I'll tell my kids
There is no need to fear
God's angels are watching over you
I think everyone in the whole wide world
Should be thankful and happy too
Knowing that God really loves us
His angels watch over me and you

Greetings

M Making melody with praise unto the Lord

U United in unity and worship

S Singing and signing together with singleness of heart

I Innovation and inspiration

C Come let us greet one another in harmony in our spirit in glorious, joyous, and blessed assurance

This is a greeting extended to everyone who walks in Jesus' joy.

Home

Where is home
It's wherever you are
You never leave home
Whether near or for
You may move away
Home goes with you
It does not stay
Memories, items, no matter what
Home is always with you it means a lot
The stories you tell, the things you do
A piece of home is always with you

Hush

Child I wish you would just shut your mouth
You just run it all the time
If you're not telling all your business
You are busy trying to run mine
Why are you so nosy
Why don't you just be quiet
Make yourself useful
Doing something worthwhile
Like going on a diet
Now I don't mean to be embarrassing
I'm not trying to hurt you . . . see
Because the person I talk about
You already know
That person happens to be me

I Ask Me Questions

What's going on
Am I here
It seems I'm nowhere
I'm out there somewhere
I do care although I am in despair
And I'm well aware
Of an unseen pressure every where
What's going on
Anguish won't leave me alone
Waiting for me to be gone
Shame on nature
And out of control hormones
That's it that is it
That's what's going on

I Didn't Forget

I thought
How can I replace
Something I know you really love and miss
I looked and asked and looked some more
Then I decided to get you this
Now, when you go to visit your friends or when they visit you
Bring it out . . . set it up
Play a game or two
I hope you will enjoy this game
Although it's not the big one
It is as close as I could get
You can carry it and put it together
Without working up a sweat
With laughter and love

This was written for my son Milton. The gift a miniature pool table

I Love To Write

I love to write. Day or night it doesn't really matter. Whether it's laughter or chatter. As long as I write. Writing takes me wherever I want or need to go. To another country or a movie show. Unlike reading a book where the pages are already full, but writing gives me no clues. Just my mind. Writing has to come from me to you.

Oft times I read and love it, but when I write I share it on a blank page, napkin empty page of a book, I even write on a written text, program or a picture I took. Writing lets my mind soar. Opens any door makes me aware of my inner self. Writing defines my mind. Erases idle time makes me feel complete whole unafraid and bold. Writing is complex make me see the facts my completeness my weakness my secrets and my fantasies. Sometimes writing frightens me. My pleasure exposed on paper for others to read. It leaves me naked, ripped to the core, yet brings me pleasure and much, much more. My writing really has no end It goes far beyond the pen, my mind keeps going when Ink and lead run out. Physical writing ends, mental writing begins over and over and over again new words and thoughts, I begin then I run to find another pencil or pen When I have no thoughts or no words will come that's when my writing will be done.

I Wish

I wish I was in a land of joy
A place where all I see
Is beautiful faces . . . bright sunny places
Where no one is angry with me
Oh how I wish I could just walk away
To a peaceful place down here
Where no one would care about worries
But have plenty time to spare
With laughter . . . no tears except
Tears of joy
I wish everyone was just as sweet
As a baby girl or boy

If

If I could take the wings of the morning
What would I do with them
If I should fly away to a distant place
Who then will care for me
If by chance I fly some place
Where great eagles nest
If I fly beyond the height of heights
Would I then find rest
If all sad memories disappear
If I have only wings of joy
If wings erased all but empty space
What then could be replaced
If my wings should break
If some unforeseen trauma shake
The foundation of mankind
Where would I land
There is an eternal plan for me
Created by the Master's hand

I'm Glad I Have a Father But I Wish I Had a Dad
Of course I have a father
Or else I wouldn't be here
But I wish I had a Dad
Dads seem to always be near
I'm glad I have a Father
Who gives me good advice
But I wish I had a Dad
Dads make good advice sound nice
I really love my Father
But a Dad would make me glad
My Father is too busy
Dads have time to cheer you up
Especially when you are sad
How can I tell my Father
To turn into a Dad
Dads never think you're too old
For hugs or to tuck you into bed
Fathers sometime seem too strict
They never seem to be at ease
Dads have time to take you for walks
In the rain with a nice cool breeze
Fathers seem to always keep promises
They hardly ever make mistakes
Dads let you know they can be wrong
Dads are there to dry your tears
Dads show you how to be strong
Fathers are so serious
Dads will let you tell a joke
Fathers say you are out of line
Dads say keep it clean
Fathers say you are punished
Dads are not always mean
I need my father
But I want a Dad
Can I make them both just one
To share, to care, to let me know when I'm wrong
To correct me . . . not provoke me
To help me to be strong

Well I guess I'll name
Him Father Dad
Two rolled into one
Then when it's my turn
I will have learned
How to be Father and Dad
To my Daughters and my Sons

Included and Excluded

Funny that when we are alone I'm included
I'm even family until
Blood family is included
Then I'm very carefully excluded
Funny how I'm Grandmother when certain ones are not around
But when reunions, weddings, funerals
And other special events come
My name is nowhere to be found
It's strange when you meet certain others
You say, "That's my family," sometimes it's even my Grandma or Mother
Oh, but when time come for you to hang out
I'm left alone and I'm just another
It's sad when I think I'm included I feel so happy . . . I'm elated
Until the real ones come around
Then I'm excluded
You even show I'm not related
Even if there's a song to be sung
Or a compliment to be sent
I'm not mentioned or even considered
Who cares how my time is spent
Included is when there's no difference in water or in blood
Excluded is when you are ashamed or afraid to let my name be heard
Excluded is when I'm never included
To share a movie, have a dinner or even a drink of something cold
Excluded, excluded oh what's the point
Am I just too slow and too old
What a terrible awful feeling
To be excluded from someone you love
What will happen when the day comes
And in a corner I'll be shoved
How can you be so blind
Can't you see how bad I'm hurting
How lonely, how painful, how selfish . . . thinking only of yourself
Your fun and your flirting
Included lasts forever
At least that's what I'm told
I never knew how to exclude someone
Because you think they are old

Excluded is knowing there are things in life we cannot share
But it's different when you only think of yourself
And never seem to care
God help me to get through these difficult times
Don't ever let me forget
To include the ones I love
No matter who I've met
When the day comes and you send me someone
Who will include me in their life
Don't let me exclude or be ashamed
To invite them into my life

It's What's Inside That Counts

What lead me to write this poem is the very realistic dream I had. It was about a minister visiting our church. It was very, very sad. This minister was sitting with the pastor, who suddenly got up and said he'd heard about my illness.

But the doctor's machine and the gifted ones
Can only see a limited amount
The Lord is the only one that can heal you inside and out
So I'm right back to the title
It's what's inside that counts.
Now outward appearance is important
Physical needs come daily too
They require attention in large amount
But when we speak of salvation
It's what's inside that counts.

It's OK To Cry

Don't hush my child
Go on and cry
That's what you do
When loved ones die
Cry my child
When you feel pain
It's OK . . . It's healing
Cry again and again
Don't be ashamed
To shed your tears
When someone leaves
Or something lost appears
It's nothing wrong
To see grown ups cry
They may not know the reason why
God designed us
To weep and mourn
In the late nights
And even the dawn
Men please cry
You are not weak
Crying only proves that you are meek
Crying expresses feelings often hidden
Some may think crying is forbidden
Remember Jesus Himself did weep
This is not a secret to keep
He wept for everyone on earth
So we weep with joy of Jesus' birth
We cry in sadness
With Jesus' death on the cross
His suffering and shame
So that we would not be lost
Cry in hope
Cry in despair
Cry in public . . . in secret
Cry anywhere
Cry for your country
The nation, the World

Cry for every boy and girl
Cry for the churches
The husbands and wives
Cry for the waste of human life
Cry for the homeless
The hungry . . . the weak
Cry for the lame
The blind the weak
Cry for the shut ins
And shut out
Cry . . . cry . . . cry with a shout
Cry . . . cry until God hears
Cry until He heals the land of fear
Cry . . . cry until He forgives
And wipes away every tear

It's Not Abuse
It's Love

They say I shouldn't have married him
They say they wish we had never met
You are always taking up for him
And he's done nothing meaningful yet
I said what do you mean
He's done plenty
He gives me lots of things
They asked what things
I said I don't remember
Well . . . yes I did pay for our wedding rings
Yes, he's going to work
I know he leaves things all over the place
But he always says I love you
And I'm so sorry I cut your face
He said, I know I was wrong . . . I don't mean no harm
I hate to cause you pain
But it's all because I love you
Even when I locked you out in the rain
Remember, I went to see you at the hospital with all those stitches
And you were all black and blue
I told the doctors, nurses, everybody
It ain't abuse
Because I really do love you
Now my darling as I stand here
Thinking of all the times we shared
I was drinking, cursing, and beating on you
I guess you thought I never cared
I sure would love to take you out
You know . . . just have some plain old fun
I wish I could turn back the hands of time
And undo what I have done
I wish someone had showed me
How this terrible thing begun
I wish someone had helped me
Not to hurt my beautiful one
I am so glad I am on my way
Of learning how to behave

To know abuse is abuse not love
What a sorrowful life I've paved
You gave me all the love you had
You, my sweetheart, my wife, my love
My love was twisted and depraved
No second chance for me
For now I stand in handcuffs and shackles
With a policeman at your grave

I've Got To Keep It Clean
I have wanted to sing and write and play
Since I was about age three
To be rich and famous
Have a lot of people see and listen to me
They tell me to be rich and famous
You gotta know all the ropes
Con the jet set . . . make fast bucks
And dab in a little dope
I say that's not true
I know what I want
That is not my dream
I'm gonna write, I'm gonna play, and I'm gonna sing
My own way which is God's way
And I'm gonna keep it clean
They say give it up . . . this world is cold
People won't dig your thing
By the time you get it together
You will be too old to sing
Your fingers will be too stiff to write
You won't hardly be able to play
Your mind will be bad your dreams a drag
Ain't nothing gonna go your way
Well, you are wrong . . . I'll get along
I'm writing and singing and I have written a play
I believe that God will see to others enjoying everything I say
This is heavenly at age seventy

Life
Life sometimes brings
Unwanted, unexpected and unhappy events
Before enjoyable time is spent
Things that may not make much sense
Life is often that way

Living In the Hood
Bye Bye black sheep
Have you any wool
This is not about a black sheep
It's about living in the hood
People talk about you
Think you're no good
But it's not all bad when you're living in the hood
Most of the houses are all boarded up
Grass no longer green
Trash lying all over the place
Not a pretty scene
Even though it's not looking good
Still not so bad living in the hood.
Men and women on the corner flirting
Children breaking open fire hydrants just to keep cool
Some running away from the law
Some hooking school
But I still say it's not all that bad in the hood
See our old and young men and women
Staring in space like they have no hope
Strung out blind as a bat
On liquor—and on dope
Begging anybody trying to score
Doing anything, anywhere, trying to get some more
But I won't take it back
It's a fact you can live in the hood
Some say this is a disgrace
I would never live in this place
People always fighting in this place
People fighting like cats and dogs
Eating anything like slopping hogs.
They just don't look like anything nice
If they're not fighting each other
They're killing each other
But I'm not sad I'm kinda glad to be living n the hood
Have you ever wondered how the hood was made
Did God create it with his hand
No, we made the hood

Truth may hurt, but the hood was made by man
I feel it in my gut it's not all dirt living in the hood
Some are poor people and living in poverty
But I ask the question who owns the property
If you really care then why aren't you here
Why haven't you been sent to rebuild, fix up, don't just collect the rent
Look at me can't you see I'm not dead I'm living in the hood
Now if you've been blest with peace and rest living in a better place
Thank God be glad don't look on the hood with disgrace
Don't leave us alone come out of your comfort zone
Visit the hood bring a pen or an empty pad
Look around write things down
Think and you will see
If you are not wise and don't open your eyes
Your neighborhood will become a hood
You will be living just like me
Living in the hood, I see the good and the blessing that God gives
It lets me see how it was then
How it is now and how again it can be
Visit the hood it's not all bad and it's not all good-it's how not where you live

Look Into My Eyes

What do you see when you look at me
Don't answer . . . look into my eyes
Can you see them . . . can you read them
Are you shocked or just surprised
If my thoughts you could read
By looking into my eyes
Oh how amazing if you could
Summarize my feelings just by looking
Into my eyes

Men, Where Are You
Mama called
Children get up . . . come to the table and eat
We can't Mama . . . it's too cold
And we have no shoes to put on our feet
Come on children come to the table
Did you wash your face
Yes, Mama but someone is missing
Where is Daddy's place
Mama looked up with a smile and said
Oh, Daddy will be back . . . he just went out for a while
Daddy, fathers, pop, where are you
Your children are crying
Your image is dying
Don't you know you are to lead, instruct, and demonstrate
It's you they will imitate
Take your wife and children by the hand
Gently show them . . . don't demand
Hold them, love them, show them the way
God through them will bless you one day

My Dear

My dear you are so cute
With your beautiful eyes
Your soft touch
No matter what I do
You never complain
You never say a word
You look at me with so much love
You snuggle up real close
My dear you always seem to be there when I need you
And when I don't
You always make me feel needed
You keep me warm
As if you are my fire and the log
My dear you are the very best
My friend forever
My dog

My Favorite is Pear
My Spirit Fruit is Faith

Faith comes by hearing, hearing the word of God. I must do what God say do to receive my heavenly reward. My favorite fruit is banana my spiritual fruit is meekness which is humility. The meek shall inherit the Earth.

When I pray I will ask the Lord give me meekness first. My favorite fruit is pear. My spiritual fruit is temperance. Temperance means self control. My favorite fruit is apples too, but my spiritual fruit is long suffering which means patience to endure. This is my duty toward one another with a heart that is kind and pure.

My favorite fruit is orange. My spiritual fruit is gentleness. This is kindness of Christ. I must show kindness everyday for this is a Christian life. My favorite fruit is peaches. My spiritual fruit is goodness. I have none of my own. God put goodness in my heart. The day I was reborn.

My Garden

If I had my very own garden, I would have each of you for a flower
Then we would watch each other grow together, hour after hour.
If some of my flowers didn't bloom for a very, very long while
I would have faith
Don't worry
And then I'd water them with a smile

My Gift
Puppy Love
I am giving you a cute little puppy
One that belongs to me
I'm sure you will enjoy it
To keep you company
What's so special about this puppy?
Well, I'm so glad you asked
He'll stay right where you put him
He doesn't run all through the house
You don't even have to feed him
Or take him to the vet
You can put him in bed
To sleep with you
He won't make a sound he is a full blood
He's a Beagle hound
This puppy can keep a secret
You can tell him whatever you like
He's clean and house broken
And he never barks back
You don't have to feed this cutie
I think I've said enough
I'll just let you see for yourself
Oh, I almost forgot
This puppy is already stuffed

My Thoughts

As I go from day to day
My thoughts often stray
These awesome thoughts keep coming back
They just won't go away
I don't have the answer
Why these things can be
But I can share
From someone who cares
The thoughts He gave to me
He holds the past, the present, and the future
In the palm of His Holy hand
No thoughts, no worries, no problem
Is too hard for the Holy Man.
When you think bad things, it's Satan
Knowing is not hard
Because good thoughts come to the same mind
These are the thoughts of God
Depend on Him
For there's no doubt about it
It has been proven over 2,000 years
We just cannot live without it

My Thoughts from Daytime Stories
As I awake in the morning I suddenly become aware of
The Secret Storm
That burns within me always reminding me of how my
Love of Life
Can keep me so occupied in my
Search for Tomorrow
I would like to remind
The Young and the Restless that
As The World Turns
There is always
The Guiding Light
To keep them, as well as myself, to see
The Edge of Night
Never stumbling and being able to stand up
Facing whatever in life we must endure

My Potential

Watch out
Try to see my potential
Helping me to see what I can be
Is very important and essential
I may be moving much too fast
The pace I'm going cannot last
This soon will be a thing of the past
Support me, push me, encourage me
As I work toward my potential.

Now That You Are Nine

Last of the single numbers
Sweet girl of nine
You are beautiful, sweet, and kind
Doing well in school
Nice friends that's cool
Be sure to keep up the good work
Girl of nine

Old Age

Old age when it does start
When things that use to be glamorous
Become distasteful and a bore
When yawning or scratching your itching head
Turns out to be a major chore
When bones are cracking and certain things start flapping
Such as chins, chests, and tummies
When old friends and even little kids
Seem to look and act like dummies
When teeth start falling
Strange voices start calling
Your glasses are not strong enough
When fruits and nuts even mashed potatoes
Make chewing troublesome and tough
Now honest . . . no joke
This is the truth about old age and when you know it's here
When you cease to care when every day is despair
You have nothing to offer or give
You have lost your will everything is uphill
There is no more reason to live
Don't feel bad
Don't be sad because you feel you are no longer young
Life has no age it goes on and on
To be enjoyed by everyone
Life is for eternity like a web that's wonderfully spun

Old age

Old? Did you just call me old
No I don't think you are cold
In fact you gave me quite a lift
Because old age is really a gift-
Think about it try and understand
Age is not given or made by man
Old age is blest by the Master's hand-
If you keep on living
One day you will see
Old age will catch you
Just like it caught me

People

I like to think of people
In a warm and pleasant way
I like to think of people
As I go from day to day
I like to think of people
Who think of what they say
I like to think of people
Who fear God and on their knees they lay
Regardless of race or creed
Or the way they think of me
I like to think of people
In a very loving way

Repeat and Retreat
What do I do when things go wrong
When happiness is hidden
And you don't have a song
What do you do when you don't belong
Retreat
What do you say when there's no place to stay
And your dreams are shattered and torn
What do you say when life is so complex
Till you wish you hadn't been born
When in your heart you want a new start
Repeat
Retreat to your secret closet
Repeat the words you feel
Retreat to that silent mental place
Retreat, repeat, be still
Repeat the positive
Retreat from the negative
Shape up without delay
Repeat all the secrets to yourself
Retreat from the scars that harm

Say You Say Me
A person afraid to come into my life
Say you say me
I have a lot to show you
It's very pleasing to the eye
Do you feel excited and anxious to see
Or are you afraid to come in a little closer to me
Don't just stand there let's start moving this way
You see you need to hear what I have to say
Say you say me
This is fun because it really doesn't say
What you or I have on our minds
Sometimes it's just that way

Stop, Look, and Listen
Stop, look at yourself
Think before you speak
Listen to another's laughter and tears
Before your own pleasures seek
Stop, listen to the sounds
That nature provides
Look around you
Nature never complains
Feel rich, feel free inside
Stop, if just for a moment each day
Look at the trees
Listen to the birds
As they sing and sway
Stop early in the morning
Look outside
Listen, what do you hear
Do we hear complaints
Do we see greed
No, nature's riches
Our eyes behold so dear
If we stop in the fields
Look at the crops
Where man his harvest sows
If we listen closely
We can hear
The harvest as it grows
Stop rushing
Take time to look
Listen everyday
Find out how we
Can better enjoy
Living nature's way

Slumber

Why do I slumber
And can not sleep
Why the tears I don't weep
My childish image has me counting sheep
I dream wide awake
I close my eyes
Rehearse all my mistakes
Mentally I rewind the time
Looking behind
Tossing and turning
Eyes burning
Is this the meaning of slumber?

Thankful

I watched people suffering
Carrying a child
Hungry, crippled and naked
Struggling for miles and miles
I could not hold back the tears
I thought I was so bad off
Worrying about things over here
Then I cried thank you Lord and dried my tears

Think About It

Your back, my back have you ever seen it? No
We see a reflection when we look in a mirror
You know why? Well I believe it's because
God in His wisdom created us this way
He wants us to know He has our backs
No matter how hard we look or how far we turn our heads
We cannot see our backs
It's amazing how God has made us

The Robe

Remember the robe
You asked for, it's still here
In my room
I didn't know that you
Would die and leave us all so soon
We just kept putting it off
Saying wait until another day
Perhaps I'll pick it up Monday
I'll be coming over your way
Because I want to have it by Sunday
You know robes are so expensive
Giving me one means a lot
Having a white robe for the choir
Is one thing I haven't got
But what's so strange, I can't explain
The joy I feel, the sadness is
Suddenly gone, that you didn't
Get the robe from me
Now you have one all your own
You see this robe unlike mine
Has been washed whiter than snow
It's been dipped in the blood of
Jesus with an everlasting glow
You will never have to borrow one
Wondering if it fits
This one is made just for you
It never wears out because Jesus Himself
Has already done the job
And like your mansion, He paid for it
He even gave you something else
He caught you up when He looked down
He said come see your mansion
Put on your robe and here
Wear your golden crown

The Shiny New Shoes

I looked at her new shiny shoes
How they clung neatly on her feet
How I longed to try them on
Wear them dance in them
Run along the street
I wonder if I ask her
Would she think I'm somewhat strange
After all she barely knows me
I doubt if she knows my name
I'll just walk right up
And ask her
If she says yes, I hope they fit
After she gets to know me
Maybe I can keep them for a bit
I spoke Hello, Hi there
May I please try on your shoes
She turned and asked, why mine
I whispered, with a sigh
I know I shouldn't have asked you
But my feet are tired and worn
She looked down and asked where are your shoes
I answered, I have none of my own
She took my hand and said you come home with me
I have lots and lots of shoes
So I went and I tried them on
I cried oh they fit perfect
Now I'm so happy
I have six pairs of shiny new shoes all my very own

The Snow Flakes
See the pretty snow flakes
Falling from the sky
On the walls and house tops
Soft and thick they lie
Look into the garden
Where the grass is green
Covered by the snow flakes
Not a blade is seen

Footnote: My Mama was born 1/15/1881 and lived 104 years. She recited this poem to me, on 2/12/84. She said she made this poem up when she was a little girl about age 9 yrs. old. Mama's Name: Telsie B. Howard

The Sun

It's so gray outside
The skies are not clear
Why . . . where is the brightness
The sun is not there
Yes it's there . . . the sun is there
Look close, real close
Right behind that cloud
Look it's in the morning
And grossly dark outside
God help me
How can that be
Wait it's not the sun
The sun is there
It's always there
Watch when the cloud passes over
Then see the sun
Right in place
Bright as God made it to be

The Thread

Oh, I was so proud of myself
After years trying to sew again
I just couldn't wait to show my curtain
To my neighbor and my friend
I kept stitching and stitching and stitching
With excitement running through my head
I could not believe I had been sewing so long
And still had not run out of thread
Well, I finally pulled my needle out
And I was so distraught
To my surprise I didn't believe my eyes
The end of my thread had no knot
The lesson I learned from this experience
Like anything you do in life
Do not jump at just the beginning
But check the outcome not once but twice
Because you don't want to make a beautiful start
Like a string of beautiful thread
Only to find you have left behind
Empty dreams and disappointments instead

The Vase
A Gift
I'm sure much
Care was put into
Making this vase
To put into a special place
So I give to you
With the very same care
To match the beauty
Of your face

The Water

I was going to see my mother
And somehow I was lost
It was raining so hard
I could not see
The street that led across
The wind was gusty
And very strong
The streets were flooded too
The water was coming from all directions
I said Lord what shall I do
The water was roaring like a lion
It was dark with dirt and mud
Red and rough with sand and clay
So angry and so gray
I started to run and cry for help
I knew I could not swim
I found a house
I knocked on the door
But no one let me in
I continued to search for shelter
From a terrible, terrible storm
I prayed I would knock on another door
And someone would be home
The water was all around me now
I began to scream
Just when I thought
My life had ended
I discovered it was only a dream

This Was No Accident
Two wonderful people have come into my life
Talented, intelligent people
A husband and a wife
I believe by God they were sent
This was not by accident
I'm thankful for special friends
Full of encouragement and support
You never know who God will send you
That's no accident

Three Girls Walking
Three Girls Talking
Hey where're you going
Who me
Yeah . . . why're you laughing
Do you see anyone else
Besides us three
But I never asked since we left home
Are we going anywhere special
Or for an ice cream cone
So hey where're we going
Why . . . can't you see
It's just three girls walking
Three girls talking
You, my friend, and me

Through My Eyes

I see us as God's flower garden
Every color, size and hue
We never know who He'll pick next
It may be me or you
When God sees one of His flowers withering
And can no longer stand the test
I see Him in His mercy saying
Come and I'll give you eternal rest
Sometimes we even question God
Why, Lord, why
Why do we have to suffer
Why do we suffer so much pain
Through my eyes
I see Him smiling down on that flower saying
Come and never suffer again

Today
What did I do today?
Nothing really oh I had a lot of calls
Basically I was alone
Spent most of the time on the phone.
Today was good and it always is
I was glad to see it no matter how I feel
I wish to be more productive
My life more fulfilled
But I accept the challenges before me
As I continue to do God's will
I'm thankful for each day I wake up
And I strive to do even more
But even when I can't
I know that God will strengthen me
And He will open doors

Welcome

What is a welcome

Acceptable, agreeable, cordial, unscorned

Greetings hospitality and open arms

Yes all seven words are meanings of welcome

As a Christian, led by God let me welcome

With these seven words

This welcome is for every man, woman, boy and girl

It includes each and everyone

Wherever these words are heard

Acceptable . . . your presence is acceptable

I am sure you will agree

We welcome you with cordial, unscorned greetings

And with Christian hospitality

So I have used six words

The seventh word I saved for last

It's the word I used with charm

Because it is an action word

Again I welcome you with an embrace and open arms

When I Was Young

When I was young
I thank God I didn't forget the old
Age has never really mattered to me
As far as spending time with an older soul
When I was young
I was always blessed
By the things the older one taught
The things I was shown
I respect the old
From the day I could recall
I have so much to offer
We have a lot locked up inside
I admit I'm not ashamed
To enjoy being with the young
This is something I'll never hide
When I was young I was told
We learn from one another
I was never too busy and I had fun
Being with my own or someone else's grandmother
Oh, how some young people change
They shove you in a corner
Come back when they have nothing else to do
If you blink your eyes or start talking
Just that fast, you're forgotten and they're a gonna
How wonderful and full life would be
If some younger wasn't so cold
If they would just stop and think if they keep living
They too one day will be old
If I had ignored the old and not seen the way they live
I don't think I could go on
What a sad time it would be
If that old one should pass on
Who said I should get a life
Never turn a page
Who said that I should only spend time
Only with people my own age
The Bible tells us to help the young
Love them, teach them, be there for them
But how can we when you are gone

When is it Time to Speak the Truth
When is it time to speak the truth
Is it as soon as you're asked
Or is it when you wish to get even
Oh this is quite a task
You speak the truth when it's expedient
Even then you had better take care
This can bring out feelings
That you did not know were there
So pick up your chin
The best way to win
Is to search your own heart within
Then you will have proof
That just knowing the truth
To face it without decree
You can't always speak it but you cannot ignore it
For the truth will set you free

When You Stray

When from God you stray
Satan has his way
What a price you pay
When from God you stray
How can we escape temptation
God has a way to remove all doubt
He is a shield and shelter
His word is our guild
He is the only way out
On this beautiful earth
With all its colors
Mountains, rivers, oceans, and sea
Birds, flowers, animals, and trees
God made this beauty for
Man throughout the land
So there is no need to stray
Ask God to hold your hand
But if you stray
As we all sometime do
Just for the asking
He will deliver you.

Who Are You

Who are you that follows me
Everywhere I go
You are there in the rain and sunshine
Even in the snow
I cannot turn without you
You follow me day and night
You don't cause any trouble
You don't argue fuss or fight
Who are you that follows me
It seems I have known you all my life
It's a wonder I don't stumble over you
Not once a day but twice
I ask once more who are you
Or does it really matter
I don't think you are going away
Because you are my shadow

Who's to Blame
Go on blame me again
I am not without sin
Take a look at yourself
Then throw your stone
If you bear some guilt
Then leave me alone
Look to right your wrongs
Do a check everyday
Make a list
See how many faults you have missed
Think before you call me a name
You say or think what I've done
Check your list, you may find you have done the same
This world would be a better place
If our own shortcoming we would face
Instead of saying I'm a disgrace
You will be singing Amazing Grace . . . .
Let's count our blessings everyday
We won't have time left to say
Look how many mistakes someone else has made
We will feel better, when we do right
Peaceful sleep will come to us each night . . . .
Courage my soul, don't leave me here alone
I didn't have the strength to go it alone
I didn't have a crutch I could leave
And I did not know how to go against the odds
I learned later it was in the cards
But I was looking to people to give me their regards
I look back over my life, with so much regret
I learned much later about what to expect
They tell me now it's up to me, I haven't seen it yet
O but I do know how to respect
Respect myself the rest falls in place
Look up and live
Look trouble right in the face
Never ever give up on my dream
Courage My Soul God is Supreme

Why are you Crying

Come here little one
Why are you crying
If you could talk would you tell me
What's on your mind
Why are you crying sweet child
I see you all the time
You smile very seldom
Most of our visit you are crying
Did someone hurt you
Do you need a change
Do you feel you are among strangers
Could it be that you are in pain
I guess I'll never know
Until you can explain
I notice when I pick you up
You start smiling again
I ask you all these questions
You did not answer at all
Someone said in a soft voice
I think little one is spoiled
I don't believe that for one minute
I think one day you will tell me
I'll step right up with a solution
With a whole lot of love in it

Why Don't You Let Me Love You
Why why don't you let me love you
Why not let me care
Why not be tender
Compassionate and true
Why not my feelings share
Why not be as close to me
As the moon is to the sun
Why can't you see the things I see
Why can't we be one
Why aren't we in harmony
Like sweet music to the ear
Why not embrace with the same good taste
Why can't you hold me near
All these whys and nots and what ifs
But if you just take the time
You would see quite clearly
We are really two of a kind

Why

Little Boy Little Girl
Why do you cry
Little boy little girl
Why such a sad sad face
Have you done wrong
Have you been harmed
Has something you love
Been misplaced
Why have you lost
Your self esteem
Why have you become so shy
Why can't you look at me anymore
Can you tell me why
Why are you so unhappy
Can you look me in my eyes
Who has hurt you, little boy little girl
I love you and I need to know why
Why, when I was a little girl
Playing in my yard
I begin to cry and cry
Why, because I had lost my favorite doll
Then there was this little boy
Who could not tell me why
But as soon as someone looked at him
He would cry and cry and cry
So one day I ask him
Why why are you ashamed
Then he finally told me
Someone called him an ugly name
So when you are not happy
Little boy little girl
And you don't know the reason why
Go to someone you love and trust
To help you work it out
To take away your fears
Dry your tears
And put away all your doubts

Winter

Oh, how I enjoyed the winter cold
Blowing blistering wind felt through my skin
Now I can remember the still trees
That once had leaves, now stripped away
Will one day when winter leaves to multiply once again

Writing

I love to write day or night
It really doesn't matter
Whether its laughter I write about
Or someone's idle chatter
It's okay as long as I write
Writing takes me wherever I need or want to go
To another country or a movie show
Unlike reading a paper or a book
Where the pages are already full
Writing gives me no clue
Just my mind
Writing has to come from me not you
Often I read and love it
But when I write . . . I show it
On an empty page, napkin, or blank page of a book
Even on the back of a picture I took

Write

I spoke to a young adult today, not a long speech just some insight. I offered encouragement and subjected how to relieve yourself when you write. You don't have to be an expert or an author of any kind, simply pick up a pen and paper write whatever is on your mind. When you do you will soon find instant relief and peace of mind. It's like a burst of sunshine releasing any chains that bind.

Your Day Will Come

I hate to see you suffer . . . your day will come
Wish you didn't come to any harm
I hope to God I'll still be living
To hold you in my arms
I know you think I don't know
What I'm talking about
I just hope I'll be around
When at last you find out
I think the reason I survive
Is because I'm not selfish
I don't do everything I should
But when you're in trouble
I'm there on the double
And I'll take the weight if I could
Oh don't you go kidding yourself
Like you have already arrived
Life is going to show you some real pain
As sure as you're alive

WORDS OF COMFORT

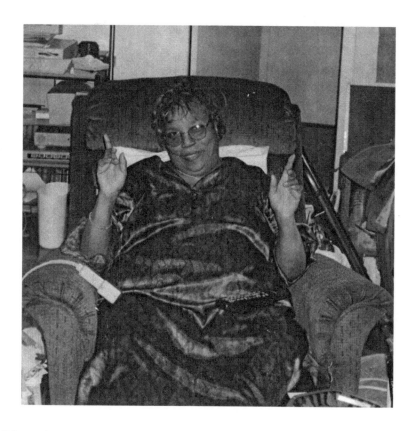

In life we have many sorrows and woes. We often struggle to find words to say. His heart is touched by our grief through life and death.

Auntie

When God loaned you to us we enjoyed having you to share through the years
We have known you, we have grown accustomed to having you near
We will always love you, we know God loved you best
We understand you now have peace
In this life you grew tired and weary
God said you are not alone so with mercy he took you in his arms
And gently carried you home

Comfort

Version 1
Life is so precious
So short yet sweet
With problems and difficulties
To meet
Life has sunshine
And its rain
Heartaches, disappointments
And many pains
This earthly life
Has its beginning and end
A time to choose between salvation
And sin
A life in Christ
Is the best of all
It prepares us when the Savior calls
When life's curtain
Is drawn
And death comes in
We can rest in Jesus
And spend eternity with Him

Comfort

Version 2

Life is so precious, short and sweet
Sometimes downs are difficult to meet
Filled with emptiness and with pain
Filled with sunshine and with rain
Filled with death and problems to solve
With heartaches, in which we all are involved
So we see a small picture of life
With bitter and also sweet
But a life with God is the best of all
He alone brings joy and peace
Now your suffering on earth is ended
Death has come at last
All pains and misery are over
All your troubles on earth has past
So sleep in Jesus, dear one
Blessed sleep
Rest in Jesus until again we meet

Death

No matter what the time may be
Whether sick or well
It seems that horrible thing called death
Arrives from the depths of hell
It comes sometimes unexpected
During the day or in the night
To the young, the old, the rich
The just, the wrong and the right
But to those of us who are in the Lord
In Him may we always see
That death has lost its vicious sting
And the grain of its victory
Knowing this is my prayer
That we will be ready to meet with our Lord and Savior
And when our time comes we will meet Him in a mansion in the sky

God is Real

Jesus took her in His arms
From all sickness, harm and danger
His grace and mercy
Will keep her in peace
For to God she is no stranger
She said I have assurance
That God would see her through
When I accepted Him into my heart
And I believe that's true
God's mercy and grace and that alone
Only His love has set me free
Never a friend so faithful
At last there is rest for me

In the Savior's Arms
For a Deceased Loved One
We know not the day
Nor the hour
When this life is hushed
In silence cold
When the curtain of time is drawn
As a thief that swiftly stole
In the twinkling of an eye
Life is over
No escape . . . how can we hide
Oh what a joy and peace
It is to know
That in the Savior's arms we abide
And in His shelter forever hide

Life

We realize God loaned you to us
But it seems like such a short while
Life goes by so swiftly
It's like the passing of a cloud.
What is life?
Life is so precious so short so sweet
Sometimes downs are difficult to meet
Filled with emptiness and with pain
Filled with sunshine and with rain
Filled with death and problems to solve
Filled with heartaches in which we all are involved.
We are a small picture of life
With bitter and sweet
But life with God is the best of all
He alone brings joy and peace
Now your suffering on earth has ended
Death has come at last
All pain and misery is over
Every trouble here has posted
Sleep in Jesus' blessed sleep
Rest in Jesus until again we meet

Missing Me

It's ok to miss me
Go ahead and cry
I know it's hard to say goodbye
Just keep on loving one another
Remember what we learned from our father and mother
Stay close and it won't be hard
And above all else
Stay close to God . . . .
Sleep on sister you deserve your rest
We really do love you
But God loves you best
With Much Love

My Mama's Gone Away
No more weeping from loneliness
No more waiting night and day
No more looking for someone who does not come
My Mama's gone away
No more watching the time
No more pains and crying
No more wondering if she's in the way
Yes, you can stop worrying
There's no need hurrying
My Mama's gone away
No more giving her care, fixing her hair
Giving her meals and her medicine, too
No trying to find excuses when you know she's looking for you
Well you can ease your mind, everything's fine
My Mama's gone away
No more suffering, bent with years
Body's tired from stress and strain
No more heartaches, feeling shut out
For reasons she cannot explain
Just take a load off yourself, no more pretending this day
My Mama, she's gone away
Now when old age comes upon you
When your time has come to go
When you have to sit back and take things you don't like
Too weak to lift your voice
When your rights have been taken, your body is shaken
When you're not even given a choice
Be sure you can say
I did my best before my Mama went away
Be sure your tears are from missing her
Be sure your conscience is clear
Be sure you have done all you could do
The years that she was here
Be able before you close your eyes
You can always truthfully say
Thank God for giving me Mama to care for and love
She's at home with Him today.

My Thoughts of Him
Or Anyone Deceased Who Knows the Lord
Let not your heart be troubled
I have finally gone on home
My troubles and tears have ended
I am safe in my Savior's arms
He is my light and my salvation
I have no need to fear
The grave has lost its victory
The sting of death is no longer near.
Just a closer walk with Jesus
To a mansion He's prepared for me
His glory lights my pathway
I have crossed that tempest sea
Lift up your heads my friends and loved ones
Prepare to meet me in the air
We can rest in peace together
And His beauty forever share
Dedicated to my husband, James E. Surles

What is Life?

Life is so precious, so short, so sweet
Sometimes downs are difficult to meet
Filled with emptiness and with pain
Filled with sunshine and with rain
Filled with death and problems to solve
Filled with heartaches, in which we all are involved
So we see a small picture of life with the bitter and with the sweet
But life with God is the best of all
He alone brings joy and peace
When your suffering on earth is ended
Death has come at last
All pains and misery are over
Every trouble here has past
Sleep in Jesus' blessed sleep
Rest in Jesus' arms until again we meet

Comfort for Someone Whose Mother Has Passed Away
My spiritual Children
I'm so sorry your mother has gone on home
Mother was your best earthy friend
She cannot be replaced by any other
Be it children, sister, or brother
No one can compare to a dear and caring mother
A mother always wants what's best for her children
She will do everything that she can do to make life better
She was also very proud of you

Just for You
Words of Comfort
I am writing this letter in the form of a poem
To bring you joy and peace
I wanted to say this in person
That was my greatest intent
But I have learned through the years it means so much
No matter where you are
How your time is spent
So here is the poem written by me
For you and your lovely wife
I thought it very appropriate
To title the poem Life

Mother's Gone
Words of Comfort
Our family circle has been broken
Another link gone from our chain
A link that can never be replaced
It's been broken again and again
You have lost other family members
Grandmother, sister, and brother
Oh how hard this pain can be dear hearts
Now that you have lost your mother
Let me share with you
My feelings about your mother, my sister, my friend
She was a sister
On whom I could depend
She had a mind to work for Jesus
She claimed Him as her own
She was talking about His goodness on Tuesday to me
On Wednesday, she went on home.
Yes, God called her from her labor
He freed her from all worry and pain
I'm not worried about my sister
In Heaven, I'll see her again
Hold fast my nephews and nieces
Run for Jesus as you have been taught
When the pain of missing your mother begins
Think of all the joy she brought
No one can ever replace your mother
But I am here for you each day
Know that God is ever present
And I'm only a phone call away
When my sister was living I didn't worry
I knew she was there for you
Now that she is gone I know you feel alone
But remember, I am here for you
Love Always

My Sister Is Not Here First Born
Words of Comfort
Your family circle has been broken
A link gone from the chain
A link that can never be replaced
Your loved one is free from pain
I did not know your loved one
But I understand she was the first born
To break the family circle
But victory is won
I hear your dear one's passing
Was grievous to family and friends
She left so many precious memories
Before coming to her journey's end
Oh how good our Savior is
To know how much we can bear
How timely He cradles us in His loving arms
And proves how much He cares . . . .
Mother, God bless her heart.
Your brothers and sisters too
The children, grandchildren other family and friends
Rest assured we are praying for you
Left with each of you is
A story you can tell
Something in her life
You can all live by
With her soul all is well
I feel I already knew her
From the beautify things you said she had done
I rejoice I knowing she ran the race, she will see his face
Yes, she ran the race
We all must run . . . .
Love Always

Passing of a Loved One
Life sometimes brings unwanted, unexpected, and unhappy events
Before enjoyable time is spent
Things that may not make much sense
Life is often that way
But I know of a better life
Where there is no fear
Never no more to shed a tear
Where heavenly gates are open wide
And Jesus stands waiting inside
When this life ends a new one begins

Sorrow
Words of Comfort
Those who have lost loved ones
I know how you must feel
Death can come so sudden
It almost doesn't seem real
I leave you with hope
There is a sweeter land we know
Let us hope to meet our loved ones
On that bright celestial shore

The Passing of a Mother

Words of Comfort
You've lost your best earthly friend
You can't replace her with another
Be it wife, children, sister or brother
None can compare to a dear sweet Mother
She always wanted the best for you
She did everything she could do
To make life better in every way
She was always proud of you
You, her one and only child
For you she would go that extra mile
Even tired she would always muscle up a smile
When she was saying something about her child
There was nothing too good for you
You could get anything she had
She always had something good to say
I don't think she ever called you bad
I know that you will miss her
More than you'll ever know
I guess you're thinking to yourself
I won't see Mother anymore
Let me share something with you
Something you can count on for sure
There is life after death
When this life is through
We hope and pray in that last day
As you know the Lord
You can be assured
You will see your Mother again

Words of Comfort
I wish you were still here with us
Losing you is like a bitter pill
I miss the times we spent talking
I could always tell you how I feel
You never seemed to worry long
You had a certain charm
You would remind me that things
Are not as bad as they seem
Then you would take me by the arm
I miss the times you took to share
In making those around you feel loved
You let us know we were needed and special
You were a blessing from above
I miss the broad smile on your face
When I fixed your favorite meal
When you made a special mixture
To enhance our taste buds still
We sure will miss that smile
When all was going well
How you could get a laugh out of everyone
With the stories only you could tell
If it was possible, for you to be here
And I speak for others too
We would say don't leave us we need you
To help brighten our days and share our cloudy ones too
But since you are gone
We must carry on
I know you would want us to
You will always be here
In our hearts you are dear
No one could ever ever replace you

Words of Comfort
In this sad hour
Of heavy hearts
Tears and oh such grief
We are deeply touched
By your loss
May God grant you
Sweet, sweet peace
Lift up your eyes
Unto the hills
From whence cometh our help
Peace and comfort
Surely will come
And ease the pain of death

Words of Comfort

When this life is over
Memories do not end
We hold them and cherish them
We repeat them again and again
We all must one day pay
So let us pray everyday
That the precious memories will last forever
And never fade away

Words of Comfort
We cannot express
What's in our hearts
Nor the sorrow that we feel
We cannot wipe away your tears
Your wounds
We cannot heal
But we can be with you in spirit
We can share your sorrow and grief
May God grant you strength and courage
May He bring your hearts relief
With deepest sympathy

Words of Comfort
To the bereaved family of
He knows just how you feel
Death can come so sudden
Sometimes it doesn't seem real
But we leave you with this hope
There's a greater land we know
Let's hope to meet
Dear _____ again
On that bright celestial shore

Words of Comfort
When our hearts are filled
With sorrow
And it seems all hope is gone
Let me tell you of a friend
That knows what must be done
There is one
Only one
Blessed, blessed Jesus
Is the one
When affliction presses the soul
Like a weight of trouble rolls
And you need a friend to help you
He's the one
God bless you & your family
In your hour of need

Words of Comfort

God be with you always
Asleep in Jesus' blessed sleep
From which none ever wakes to weep
A calm and undisturbed repose
Unbroken by the last of foes
O how sweet
To be for such a slumber meet
With holy confidence to sing
That death has lost its vicious sting

Words of Comfort
When our hearts are filled with sorrow
When it seems all hope is gone
Let me tell you of a friend named Jesus
Who knows what can be done
He is the one in this sad time
Who can and will bring you through
The days and nights that lie ahead
Because he cares for you

Words of Comfort
From One Who Cares
The time has come
For me to say
I know how you must feel
The journey's been long and tedious
The race mostly uphill
Then God in His grace and mercy
Saw time to bring relief
Even in your time of sorrow, pain and grief
I know you'll miss your loved one
But suffering has its end
May you find peace and comfort
In Christ Jesus and your friends

Words of Comfort
To An Only Child

I
Dear one, I know just how you feel
Because your best earthly friend is gone
Because wife, children, sister or brother
There's no one to replace
A dear sweet mother

II
She wanted the very best for you
She did everything that she could do
To bring you up better than
Most of the people you knew
She would say I'm very proud of you

III
You, her one and only child
For you she went the extra mile
Even tired she would muster up a smile and say
There's nothing too good for my child
I know you will miss her
More than you'll ever know
I guess you're saying to yourself
I won't to see mother anymore

IV
My child let me share something with you
Something you can count on that's sure
There is life after death
When this life is through

V
There is someone you can turn to
A friend like no other
This friend I recommend to you
Is closer than a mother . . . .
You can give Him your heart any time

He will be with you to the end
He's waiting to save and comfort you
Yes, my child, Jesus is that friend
You will see mother again

Words of Comfort
To Mama

My Child is Gone
God has laid me down
To sleep
My Mama covered me up
No more will I suffer
Or drink from the bitter cup
Death has no more hold on me
God's mercy has set me free
I have no pains, no chains, no heartaches
The Lord have given me victory
Mama please tell my brothers and sisters
Tell all my loved ones and friends
My life on earth has ended
Now my new life with Christ begins
Thank you Mama for all you did for me
Though sometimes I failed the test
Thanks for your love, tears, patience, and prayers
You always gave me your best.
If I could speak a word right now
Or hear you pray again
I'd say mama please don't cry for me
I am free, free, free from this world of sin
I know I will be missed
I know many tears will fall
But everyone, even I, Mama
Must answer when God calls
Take care don't worry Mama
Remember you covered me up
I'm safe in the fold
Away from the cold
God knew when I had enough
Mama, I just feel if your child was still here with you he would say these words.

Words of Comfort

When God loaned you to us
We enjoyed having you to share
Through the years we have known you
We have grown accustom to having you near
We will always love you the most
In this life you grew tired and weary
God knew and with mercy He called you home

Words of Comfort
I write these words for you
Your _____ cannot hear them
What can I tell
My niece (loved one)
A young widow
And mother too
How can I say all the right words
What can I really do
I could tell her all about life's ups and downs
All the trials we must endure
The joys and sorrows
The heartaches and pains
That sometimes we all go through
I could tell her oh try not to worry
Everything will be fine
We are all right here for you
Just call us any time
All of these things I could tell her
And every one of them are true
But most of all I want to tell her
What all of us must do
We must get to know someone
Who can cure the pain
And mend the broken heart, too
He knows about your hurt
He knows just how you feel
He knows just how suddenly
Death can come
He will sweeten that bitter pill
He will teach us how to help you
He will give us what to say
He understands your tears and fears
He will wipe them all away
He can see inside that broken heart
And search that troubled mind
He will show you how to face tomorrow
And put yesterday behind
Just trust Him, ask Him to help you

Tell Him what He already knows
He will lead you, guide you
And take you where you need to go
I'm telling you about the Savior
Jesus Christ, the Son of God
You can depend on Him
He'll be your friend
Even now when it seems so hard
Someday death will come to us all
But there is eternal life
To all who accept and believe in Him
The Savior, Jesus Christ
I love you and
I share your sorrow

Words of Comfort
To An Only Child

Dear one I know just how you feel a friend is gone, because wife, children, sister, or brother. There's no one to replace a dear sweet mother.

She wanted the very best for you, she did everything that she could do. To bring you up better than most of the people you knew. She would say, I'm very proud of you.

You're her only child for you she went that extra mile, even tired she would muscle up a smile and say there's nothing to good for my child.

I know you will miss her more than you will ever know. I guess you 're saying to yourself, I won't see mother any more.

My child let me share something with you, something you can count on that's sure there is life after death when this life is thru. There is someone you can turn to, a friend like no other this friend I recommend to you.

Is closer than a mother you can give him your heart anytime. He will be with you to the end. He is waiting to save and comfort you. Yes my child Jesus is that friend. You will see mother again.

THANK YOU

I say to you from my heart thank you for your love and support. I thank you for coming into my heart and my mind through "Dot's Conner from My Heart"
May God Bless and Keep You

Love Always Momma Doris

Mommy you are Love "Thank You"

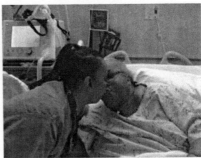

Thank You

Thank you my beautiful women
For helping me to get through
You were a part of my recovery
Your kindness was helpful too
Words are mere expressions
Of how I truly feel
Your prayers, gifts and calls
Kept me company while I was ill
Thank God for restoring my body
Thank you for taking a part
All praise, glory and honor to the Heavenly Father
All of you will remain in my heart

Thank You

God has granted me the principle to say Thank you once again.
Your prayers, calls and many kind expressions has shown you are my
Christian friends. Thank you for being there for me. Iit is my prayer that
God will continue to bless you and keep you in his care.

Thank You
For this I'll always be grateful
Your love has shown you care
If I ever have the choice to
Return these kind expressions and love
Just know that I will be there

Thank You

A card cannot express
The kindness you have shown
You shared my loss and sorrow
As if they were your own
Your prayers and kind expressions
Proud you are people of God showing Jesus' love
I'm sending words of gratitude
May you be showered with blessings from above

Thank You

Thank you one and all
For your prayers, cards, words of encouragement
And your telephone calls
You helped me to a speedy recovery
Brought sunshine
During my pains
Each day you sent a rainbow of love
To prove that happiness comes to even me
And my life isn't always rain

Thank You

Words cannot express
The kindness you have shown
You help me through my illness
As if it was your very own
No one could ever feel
More blessed than I am today
The compassion, the prayers
And all the expressions
You have sent my way
What God said is His word
Is what my family has done
You fed me, prayed for me
Oh I thank you everyone
You make me feel loved and special
For this I know God is pleased
It is truly a gift from above
This love and support is a great comfort
My spirit is greatly relieved

Thank you

I thank you for your kindness
Thanks for your considerate deeds
Thanks for your caring and your quick response
During my time of need
People like you are very rare
In numbers you are few
The calm you've shown
When you answer the phone
Handling the stress and strain
Gives you an inward beauty, too
I hope these words encourage you
And all those you hold dear
May the warmth you send
To so many homes
Remain in your hearts this Holiday season
And throughout the coming year

Thank You

There are so many times I wish I could embrace each and everyone of you. I wish I had arms long enough to hug all of you at the same time. Your visits, cards, calls, even your thoughts. Your prayers for me mean so much. Sometimes thank you seems so small, but I remember little things mean a lot.

Thank You My Family

I think you are really neat
I love the way you show your love
By bringing me good things to eat
Mary James, Sandra Kelly, Catherine Richardson, too
These sisters are really something
With their piping hot homemade delicious chicken and dumplings
I can't forget my son Milton and my Christian son
They came just when I was ready
Collard greens, corn, grilled chicken
And their awesome meatballs and spaghetti
Now Lillian McKenzie and Joyce Howell
Sweet as a little lamb
Brought me string beans, potato bread and yams
Oh yeah and a tender melt in your mouth ham
My daughters Freda and Gaynell
Gaynell a sweet little turtle dove
Never a day without a big Italian sub
Freda hardly missed a time on any given day
To call and say I'll be right over with something from Subway
Gaynell let me tell you something I really miss
Although you claim you cannot cook you make delicious tuna fish
Fruits, nuts, candy and pie
Even apple strudel
To the taste and joy I find
When Grandson Milton and Granddaughter Kayla
Fix me hot Oodles of Noodles
All the things I've listed above
But no way can they compare
To the spiritual food I have received
Through communion and fervent prayer
My pastor prayed for me
Deacons came and gave me communion
Brothers and sisters came to visit
What a blessed reunion

Words of Thanks
Dearest Friend
Words cannot express
The kindness you have shown
The way you shared our problems
As if they were your own.
We will ever be grateful
For your words of prayer
We appreciate your generous deeds
Somehow you knew
And you were there
In our time of needs
Our prayers and gratitude
You will always have
Each time I thank God
For a friend such as you
Your love, concern and friendship
Is very rare
And found only in a few
With God's blessings and our sincerity

In God's vast universe one small corner is enough space for me to bring happiness to your heart and smiles to your faces. I am so thankful to the Lord for this. You see He gave me a gift; one I do not take lightly. The greatest gift of all—the art of writing. From a child I have written and it has always been my dream to pen my words to paper. It's been extremely difficult at times coming up with so many siblings and so many problems to find a quiet time to write (Smile). I am the baby of 16 children. But anyhow by the grace of God I found a way.

I love to write. Day or night it doesn't really matter. Whether it's laughter or chatter, as long as I write. Writing takes me wherever I want or need to go, to another country or a movie show, unlike reading a book where the pages are already full, but writing gives me no clues. Just my mind, writing has to come from me, that's how I reach you.

Often times I read and love it, but when I write I share it on a blank page, a napkin, a piece of cardboard, empty page of a book. I even write on a written text, program or a picture I took. Writing lets my mind soar. Opens any door, makes me aware of my inner self. Writing defines my mind, erases idle time, makes me feel complete, whole, unafraid and bold.

Writing is complex and makes me see the facts—my completeness, my weakness, my secrets and my fantasies. Sometimes writing frightens me. My pleasures and innermost feelings, thoughts and emotions exposed on paper for others to read. It leaves me naked, ripped to the core, yet brings me pleasure and much, much more. My writing really has no end it goes far beyond the pen; my mind keeps going when ink and lead run out. Physical writing ends, mental writing begins over and over and over again. New words and thoughts I begin then I run to find another pencil or pen. When I have no thoughts or no words will come, that's when my writing will be done.

Before I could put words in a sentence, before I could put pen to paper, before I could properly form a letter or make a rhyme, I wanted to grow up and do three things in life. I wanted to have children, sing God's praises and then write. God has blessed me with two wonderful children, Gaynell Colburn and Milton Hall, Jr., now adults. Once in a while I am blessed to sing and now I have an opportunity to share some of my writings with the world.

Through my many illnesses, trials and tribulations and through long-suffering I learned from my mother how to be an anyhow person. That is something that I have passed on to my daughter and something that I still use in my everyday walk with the Lord. My passion is to write. Writing is a great relief for me even in my darkest hour, throughout my long suffering, throughout all the trials. No matter what's going wrong my writing always makes things go right. So I thought I'd share this with you and hopefully you can see through me no matter what you are going through anyhow you can write, you can sing, you could pray, you can trust in the Lord and you can go forward. Let my book from this lady, a senior citizen, give you the inspiration and the encouragement that you might need to become an anyhow person.

Dot's Corner will help you to see that you are never too old or too slow or too poor or too weak to strive for your life's goals. May God Bless and Keep you.

May my writings be a blessing to you. Through it all I learned to depend solely on God.

Sincerely yours,

Momma Doris

Doris Howard Surles

On May 2, 2009 at 11:40 am Momma Doris Howard Surles departed this life to go home with the Lord. She through long suffering, endured, smiled, laughed, talked, and had her sound right mind until her last minutes on Earth. I, her daughter Gaynell Colburn, would like to dedicate once again from my heart and from Momma Doris' heart her life's work with love and respect to each of you. Through many months, days, weeks, she endured severe pain and agony. My mother truly personified what she taught every day and that's how to be an "anyhow person". Smile anyhow, pray anyhow, thank the Lord anyhow, and give everything to Him that you can't bear anyhow. Mommy truly was an "anyhow person" as her mother was and as she tried to teach me to be and how I hope this book will help you be an "anyhow person".

One of Mommy's favorite sayings was "I don't own it. Give all to Him." When the doctors brought her bad news, that she was terminal, that she only had a few months left, she would put it in her "give away bag". Give it to God. With a big old heavy give away bag, you don't try to carry it or hold it, you give it to God.

In closing I say to you that God could not have given me a better gift in life than my mommy. I thank Him every day for that blessing, for her life, for the time we shared which was priceless. Thank you Lord for giving me my Mommy.

I love you with all my heart Mommy.

Gaynell Colburn

Why do I write?

I write because it brings me joy and
God gives me the ability to pen words to paper
In the midst of my pain I write
In sorrow I write
In the midst of my totally devastating journey of illness I write
For all the days I wanted to sing and was not allowed to I write
When I look in to the pain in my daughter's eyes I then write
Through long suffering I write
In the midst of my life's storms I write
In the good times I write and happy times I write
From a child when I needed to get away I write
I write because it makes me happy
Why do I write? My heart sings out the words from my mind
In this my life's writings there will be expressions and emotions
So as you look into the corner you will find
Pieces of my heart pen to paper
From the corners of my mind I write.

Breinigsville, PA USA
14 January 2010
230750BV00001B/51/P